A Taxi Driver's Guide to LONDON

A TAXI DRIVER'S Guide to London

by S. Raingold

LONDON
W. Foulsham & Co Ltd
New York Toronto Cape Town Sydney

W. Foulsham & Co Ltd
Yeovil Road, Slough, Bucks., England

Illustrations in the text by
Richard Munday
Kathleen McDougall

Maps by Claus Henning

IBSN 0-572-00867-8

Made and printed in Great Britain by
Redwood Press Limited
Trowbridge, Wiltshire

This book is dedicated
to my wife,
son and daughter

Acknowledgements

I offer my grateful thanks to the staff of the Ealing Reference Library and to Mr C. H. Gibbs-Smith of the Victoria and Albert Museum, as well as to all the staff and officials of libraries, institutions, hospitals, clubs and hotels who have helped me in my research; and to the many passengers who have always been most helpful.

The maps on pages 232 and 233 are by kind permission of Geographers' A–Z Map Co. Ltd.

How to use this book

The material is arranged alphabetically, covering places, people and topics, and has two comprehensive indexes, one of people, the other of places and subjects. Any place of particular interest referred to in the text is printed in small capitals. The book contains maps of Central London with a key (see pp. 219–231), while the references in brackets in the text are to the more detailed maps of the *Geographers' A to Z Atlas of London*.

A

Actors' Church St Paul's, Covent Garden, Bedford Street [3E 60d] was originally built in 1635 by Inigo Jones for the Duke of Bedford, who intimated that he wanted something to the design of a barn; in return he got the most dignified sacred barn in the country. It was called the Actors' Church because at one time a number of its parishioners were performers at the Covent Garden and Drury Lane theatres. It was rebuilt by Thomas Hardwick in 1798 after a fire.

Adams, John Quincy (1767-1848) Son of John Adams, America's second President. On July 26th 1797 he married Louisa Johnson at All Hallows by the Tower, Eastcheap, the same church in which William Penn, founder of Pennsylvania, was baptised. Appointed Ambassador to The Hague, then to Berlin and in 1815 to the Court of St James. In 1824 he was elected President of the United States (the sixth) and held this post until 1828.

Adams, John (1735-1826) American statesman, a member of the committee that framed the Declaration of Independence. From1785 to1788 he was ambassador to Britain and in 1797 succeeded George Washington as president of the USA. He lived at 9 Grosvenor Square, Mayfair [3F 60b].

Adelphi [4F 60d] The Greek word '*adelphoi*' means 'brothers' and the area south of the Strand near Charing Cross station was named after the four Adam

Admiralty Arch, viewed from Buckingham Palace.

brothers who laid it out in 1768-74 on the site of Durham House, the town house of the bishops of Durham. Their scheme formed the first embankment on the Thames, but little of its original character is now left. However, the names ADAM STREET, JOHN ADAM STREET and ROBERT STREET are still reminders of the brothers. Robert Adam is buried in WESTMINSTER ABBEY.

Admiralty Arch [1D 62d] The gateway that leads from TRAFALGAR SQUARE to the MALL and Buckingham Palace was built in 1910 as a memorial to Queen Victoria to Sir Aston Webb's designs.

Agnew's Galleries Famed for watercolour exhibitions, particularly of English watercolours and drawings of the eighteenth and nineteenth centuries. The galleries owe their origin to Thomas Agnew (1794-1871), who in 1810 joined the art business of Vittore Zanetti in Manchester and seven years later became a partner. The present galleries at 43 OLD BOND STREET [4B 60c] (built on the site of an old coaching yard) were opened in 1876.

Albany, Albany Ct. Yd., Piccadilly [4C 60c] Built in 1770 from Sir William Chambers's designs for Lord Melbourne, who sold it to the Duke of York and Albany in exchange for £10,000 and a mansion in Whitehall; the Duke lived there from 1791 to 1802. In 1802 the establishment was converted into bachelor apartments. Canning and Gladstone (prime ministers) and Lord Byron (poet) were among its many distinguished residents.

Albany Apartments.

Albemarle Street, Piccadilly [4B 60c] Built on the site of Albemarle House, the residence of General Monk, first Duke of Albemarle (1608-70). Monk was a soldier and politician who was responsible for restoring Charles II to the throne, and the founder of the Coldstream Guards. In 1652 he married Nan Clarges, a seamstress, at ST GEORGE THE MARTYR, BOROUGH HIGH STREET. In 1665 he resigned his naval command to tend Londoners suffering from the plague.

Albert Embankment [1F 77] Between Lambeth and Vauxhall Bridges. It was opened on 24 November 1869 and named after the Prince Consort. It took three years and four months to construct and is half a mile long.

Albert Hall [2B 62a] Built 1867-71 to the designs of Captain Francis Fowke on a site in KENSINGTON GORE purchased with the proceeds of the 1851 Exhibition, which was held in Hyde Park. It was opened by Queen Victoria and remains as a memorial to Prince Albert, the Prince Consort. The hall holds 8,000 people and is the home of the Promenade

The Thames viewed from the Albert Embankment.

Concerts every summer. The organ, with nearly 10,000 pipes, is one of the largest in Britain.

Albert Memorial [1B 62a] Designed by Sir Gilbert Scott and erected in KENSINGTON GARDENS in 1861 as a national memorial to Prince Albert. The book in his hand represents the catalogue of the 1851 Exhibition.

Albert, Prince Francis Charles (1819-61) Younger son of Ernest, Duke of Saxe-Coburg-Gotha, cousin of Queen Victoria, whom he married on 10 February 1840 in the CHAPEL ROYAL, ST JAMES'S PALACE. He sponsored the Exhibition in 1851 in Hyde Park, and was given the title of Prince Consort in 1857. He died of typhoid fever. Statue in HOLBORN CIRCUS; ALBERT MEMORIAL in KENSINGTON GARDENS.

Aldersgate, City Derives its name from the alder trees that grew round the gate. The gate is presumed to have been built by Aldrich the Saxon and stood on or near the present junction of ALDERSGATE STREET and GRESHAM STREET [2D 61b]. It was removed in 1761. The junction of ALDERSGATE STREET and GOSWELL ROAD [1D 61b] marks the northern end of the City.

Aldwych, Strand [3F 60d] Opened by Edward VII and Queen Alexandra on 18 October 1905; it is presumed to have taken its name from an old settlement ('*Ald Wic*') which stood on or near this site in Saxon times.

Alexandra Palace, Muswell Hill [1D 29] Known as the 'Alley Palley'. It was opened in 1873 and named after Queen Alexandra, wife of Edward VII. Within two weeks of opening it was gutted by fire, but was rebuilt and reopened in 1875. During the First World War it housed Belgian refugees, and later became an internment camp for the Germans. It has been used for concerts, horse racing (track closed in 1970) and so on, and by the BBC for radio and television transmissions.

Alexandra, Queen (1844-1925) Wife of Edward VII, eldest daughter of Christian IX of Denmark; called the 'Danish Rose'. She took a great interest in the London hospitals and gave support to the widows and orphans of those who fell in the Boer War. She was instrumental in founding the Alexandra Rose Collection, one of the earliest flag days, the proceeds of which go to hospitals. There is a monument to her on the wall of MARLBOROUGH HOUSE (*see main entry*).

Allenby, Edward Henry (1861-1936) Commander of the Allied Forces in Palestine, captured Jerusalem and ended Turkish resistance; made field marshal and viscount in 1919. He lived 1928-36 at 24 WETHERBY GARDENS, Earls Court [4A 62a], and is buried in WESTMINSTER ABBEY.

Amen Corner [4C 92] Some streets round ST PAUL'S CATHEDRAL are believed to have taken their names from pre-Reformation Roman Catholic processions; according to this tradition the 'Hail Mary' was said in AVE MARIA LANE and 'Amen' in AMEN CORNER (*See Paternoster Row*).

American Bishops The first were consecrated in 1787 in LAMBETH PALACE (*see main entry*), the official residence of the Archbishops of Canterbury.

American Chapel The name given to GROSVENOR CHAPEL, in SOUTH AUDLEY STREET, Park Lane [4F 60b], which was built for Sir Richard Grosvenor in 1730; here during the Second World War the American armed forces held divine service.

American Church CHRIST CHURCH, KENNINGTON [2A 63a], at the junction of Westminster Bridge Road and Kennington Road, was built in 1876 for the congregation of the Surrey Chapel. It was called the American Church because embedded in its spire is the Stars and Stripes. Its tower, called the Lincoln Tower, was built with American funds as a memorial to Abraham Lincoln (*see main entry*).

American Cotton The CHELSEA PHYSIC GARDEN in ROYAL HOSPITAL ROAD, Chelsea [1C 76], was founded by the Society of Apothecaries in 1673. In 1721 Sir Hans Sloane (*see main entry*) presented the freehold to the Society on condition that they send fifty new plants every year for a number of years to the Royal Society. Cotton plants were brought from India and cultivated. Then, in 1732, they were sent from this garden to Carolina in the United States, thereby helping to create the American cotton industry.

American Philanthropist George Peabody (1795-1869), an American, came to London in 1837, worked as a stockbroker and made a fortune. He donated large sums of money to Harvard University and built the Peabody Museum in Boston, Massachusetts. In 1862 he erected the Peabody Estates in London, housing many working-class families. As a result of his good work, Queen Victoria offered him a baronetcy, which he refused to accept. He died at 80 EATON SQUARE, Belgravia [3F 62b]. Monument in Royal Exchange Avenue, Threadneedle Street, by the Bank of England.

America's London Bridge When London Bridge was opened in the Arizona Desert in the USA on 9 October 1971 the Lord Mayor of London, Sir Peter Studd, and a party of 200 people flown over from Britain were present. The bridge, reassembled from

10,246 pieces in two years, was bought for £1 million by an American oil company, which at the time of negotiations was under the impression that it was purchasing Tower Bridge.

Anderson, Elizabeth Garrett (1836-1917) In 1865 she was admitted to the Society of Apothecaries where she obtained her degree and became the first English woman doctor and physician. In 1908 she was appointed Mayor of Aldeburgh, Suffolk and became the first woman to hold mayoral office. She lived at 20 UPPER BERKELEY STREET, Edgware Road [3E 60b]. The ELIZABETH GARRETT ANDERSON HOSPITAL, EUSTON ROAD [4E 45] bears her name.

Angel, Islington [4B 46] Derives its name from the Angel Tavern which stood in HIGH STREET, ISLINGTON and which was established in the seventeenth century. It used to be a favourite resort for farmers, salesmen and graziers, who wined and dined here before going to SMITHFIELD MARKET (*see main entry*).

Anglo-American Military Formed about 1537, under the title of the Guild or Fraternity of St George, the HONOURABLE ARTILLERY COMPANY, CITY ROAD, MOORGATE [4B 46], and is the oldest military body in Britain. In 1638 a Mr R. Keayne, a member of the Company, founded the ancient Honourable Artillery Company in Boston, Massachusetts. This Company fought against the British in the War of Independence and is the oldest military body in America.

Anne, Queen (1665-1714) Born in ST JAMES'S PALACE (*see main entry*), daughter of James II. She married Prince George of Denmark; they had seventeen children but none survived to maturity. On the death of William of Orange in 1702, she became queen and reigned for twelve years. During her reign Marlborough won his outstanding victories at Blenheim, Ramillies, Oudenarde and Malplaquet in the War of the Spanish Succession. QUEEN ANNE'S GATE, St James's Park [2D 62d] commemorates her name. She is buried in WESTMINSTER ABBEY. Statue in forecourt of ST PAUL'S CATHEDRAL.

Antiseptic Peer John Lister (1827-1912) was the first English surgeon to use antiseptics and the first member of his profession to receive a peerage. He discovered that carbolic acid was an antiseptic, invented absorbent dressings of sterilized gauze and fought for greater cleanliness in the care of patients. He lived at 12 PARK CRESCENT [1A 60c], near where his memorial now stands in PORTLAND PLACE, W.1.

Apothecaries Take their name from *apotheke*, a Greek word meaning 'storehouse'. They were originally tradesmen who sold drugs and prescribed medicines. In 1670 the company built APOTHECARIES' HALL in BLACKFRIARS LANE, Queen Victoria Street [3C 61a]. Today the society is still an examining body that grants certificates to chemists, midwives and surgeons.

Apsley House, Hyde Park Corner [3C 60] Built in 1778 for the second Earl of Bathurst (Baron Apsley) to designs by Robert Adam. In 1817 the Duke of Wellington (*see main entry*) bought it. After the Duke had been stoned by a mob here in 1831, he erected iron shutters (which were, however, removed in 1856). The house was damaged by bombs during the Second World War. In 1947 the seventh Duke of Wellington presented it to the nation, and on 19 July 1952 it was opened to the public as the Wellington Museum.

Arches, The Flanagan and Allen, the two comedians famed for their Crazy Gang shows, in 1926 composed

Apsley House. Designed by Robert Adam.

and first sang the song 'Underneath the Arches'; they got their inspiration for this from the arches between VILLIERS STREET and CRAVEN STREET, Strand [4E 60d].

Arlington Street, Piccadilly and adjacent **Bennet Street** [4B 60c] Named after Henry Bennet, Earl of Arlington (1618-85) who fought under Charles II with the Royalist army and was wounded at Andover. His residence was Arlington House, which was demolished in 1703 and its site acquired for Buckingham House, which later became BUCKINGHAM PALACE (*see main entry*).

Arne, Thomas (1710-78) Composer. At the age of twenty-three he composed *Rosamond*, his first opera. He also wrote oratorios and theatre music but he is remembered chiefly for his songs 'Under the Greenwood Tree' and 'Rule Britannia' (*see also National*

Anthem). He was the first to introduce women's voices into oratorio choruses, in 1773. He lived in a house on the site of 215 KING'S ROAD, Chelsea [1B 76], and is buried in ST PAUL'S CHURCH, COVENT GARDEN. ARNE STREET, Covent Garden [4E 60d] commemorates his name.

Arnold, Matthew (1822-88) Poet and critic, professor of poetry at Oxford 1857-67. His poems include 'The Forsaken Merman', 'The Scholar Gipsy' and 'Sohrab and Rustum', and he also wrote studies on education. He lived at 2 CHESTER SQUARE, Belgravia [3A 62c].

Art and Argument at Schomberg House Thomas Gainsborough (1727-88), portrait and landscape painter, painted fifteen portraits of George III and the royal family. His best-known works are 'The Blue Boy', 'The Harvest Wagon' and portraits of David Garrick and Mrs Siddons. He lived and died at SCHOMBERG HOUSE, 80 PALL MALL [1C 62c] and is buried in ST ANNE'S CHURCH, KEW. Schomberg House was the property of the Duke of Schomberg, one of the generals who came to England with the Prince of Orange. It was said of the Duke that he would argue with anyone and everyone except his enemies.

Artillery Lane, Bishopsgate [2A 61c] Laid out on an artillery ground known as Teasel Close. Here the crossbow-makers trained men, and gunners from the Tower of London came to practise.

Artillery Row, Victoria Street [3C 62c] Built on an area where the residents of Westminster practised shooting on a large mound of turf known as the Butts.

Auctioneers The world's oldest firm for fine art auctions was opened in 1766 by James Christie at

125 PALL MALL [1C 62c]. In 1803 the founder died, and twenty-three years later the firm moved to its present quarters at 8 KING STREET, St James's Street [1C 74]. Sotheby's of 34 NEW BOND STREET [3A 60c] opened their auction rooms in 1744, but they did not deal with fine arts at that time.

Austen, Jane (1775-1817) Novelist. Her best-known works are *Emma*, *Sense and Sensibility*, *Northanger Abbey*, *Mansfield Park*, *Persuasion* and *Pride and Prejudice*. She lived with her brother from 1814 to 1815 at 23 HANS PLACE, Pont Street, S.W.1. [3E 62b].

Australia House At the junction of the STRAND and the ALDWYCH [3F 60d], built 1911-18 by A. M. MacKenzie and A. G. R. MacKenzie as the general headquarters in London of the Commonwealth of Australia. The bronze group of the sun horses above the door is the work of Sir Bertram MacKennal. In 1950 Australia presented the HOUSES OF PARLIAMENT (*see main entry*) with the Speaker's Chair, which is at the northern end of the House of Commons.

Francis Bacon, philosopher and author. Thought by some to have been responsible for some of the works attributed to William Shakespeare.

B

Bach, Johann Christian (1735-82) Composer. Youngest son of Johann Sebastian Bach. He came to London in 1759 and was later appointed musical director to Queen Charlotte, wife of George III. He wrote several operas including *Orione* and *La Clemenza di Scipione*. He is buried at St Pancras Old Church, Pancras Road, King's Cross [3E 45].

Bacon, Francis (1561-1626) Statesman and philosopher. Born in York Place, Strand [3E 60d], baptized in the old St Martin-in-the-Fields, Trafalgar Square. He was instrumental in setting up the Apothecaries' Charter, which is still in use today. He wrote *The Advancement of Learning*, *Essays* and *The New Atlantis*. He was appointed Lord Chancellor in 1618, but three years later was charged in the House of Lords with taking bribes and dismissed from office. He lived for nine years at Canonbury Tower, Canonbury Place [2B 46] (now the Towers Theatre). Statue in South Square, Gray's Inn, Holborn [2A 61a].

Bagehot, Walter (1826-77) Economist. Educated at University College, London. From 1860 until his death he was editor of *The Economist*. Author of *Lombard Street* and *The English Constitution*. He lived at 12 Upper Belgrave Street, Belgravia [2F 62b].

Baker Street Built in about 1799, the abode of Sherlock Holmes, the famous fictional detective. The street is named after Sir Edward Baker, who helped the Portman family to develop their London estate.

Baldwin, Stanley (1867-1947) First Earl of Bewdley. Some called him 'Honest Stan'. In 1908 he entered Parliament as a Conservative MP. He was three times prime minister: in 1923, 1926-9 and 1935-7. He handled the General Strike of 1926 and the abdication of Edward VIII in 1936. He lived at 93 EATON SQUARE, Belgravia [3F 62b].

Balfe, Michael William (1808-70) Irish operatic composer and singer who began composing at the age of nine. His operas include *The Bohemian Girl.* His songs, such as 'Killarney' and 'Come into the Garden', are still very popular today. He lived at 12 SEYMOUR STREET, Marble Arch [3D 60b].

Baltic Exchange, 26 St Mary Axe, City [3A 61c] This has little to do with the Baltic. It was formed by the amalgamation of two Exchanges, one of which was named after the Virginia and Baltick Coffee House. This Exchange, rebuilt in 1903 and enlarged in 1956, is the headquarters of traders and shipping brokers dealing in grain, coal and other floating commodities.

Bank Guard Every evening from 1780 until 26 March 1962 a detachment of Guards marched from Chelsea or Wellington Barracks to the BANK OF ENGLAND to act as guard during the night. This march took an hour. After 26 March 1962 the march only took place at weekends and the final one occurred on 8 April 1962.

Bank Holidays John Lubbock (1834-1913), Member of Parliament for Maidstone and London University 1870-1900, was responsible for the Shop Hours Regulation Act and, in 1871, the Bank Holiday Act.

This made Easter Monday, Whit Monday, the first Monday in August and Boxing Day 'Bank Holidays'. (In 1964, the last instead of the first Monday in August was created Bank Holiday.) Lubbock was born at 29 Eaton Place, Belgravia [3F 62b].

Bank of England [3F 61b] Called 'The Old Lady of Threadneedle Street'. Founded in 1694 by a Mr Paterson to assist William of Orange with finance for his war against France. Before 1734, when the building was erected on its present site to George Sampson's designs, the directors conducted their business in the Mercers' and, later, the Grocers' Livery Hall. The bank was redesigned by Sir John Soane and nationalized in 1946. THREADNEEDLE STREET is said to have been originally called Three Needle Street, from the shield of the Needle-Makers' Company.

Banks Martin's Bank in LOMBARD STREET [3F 61b], founded in 1563, is said to be the oldest bank in the country.

The overseas branch of the Midland Bank at the junction of GRACECHURCH STREET and FENCHURCH STREET [3F 61b], opened in 1962, is the largest foreign banking unit in the world.

Child's Bank, FLEET STREET [3B 61a], dates back, according to some of its records, to 1640. Among its patrons were Nell Gwyn, Oliver Cromwell (*see main entry*) and John Dryden (*see Dryden Street*). In 1729 this bank issued printed banknotes, the first bank in London to do so. It is credited with being the oldest private bank in the country.

Banks, Sir Joseph (1743-1820) Botanist. Born in ARGYLL STREET, Oxford Circus [3B 60c]. In 1768 he sailed with Captain Cook on his voyage round the world. He named the area where he discovered a number of then unknown plants Botany Bay President of the Royal Society and a founder of the Botanical Gardens at Kew [1C 72]. His home, 32 Soho Square [2D 60c], was famous as a scientific centre.

Barbecue London's first known barbecue took place below London Bridge in 1683 when an ox was roasted on the Thames, which was completely frozen at the time.

Barbican, City [1D 61b] Presumed to have got its name from a Roman tower attached to the city wall. From here sentries gave warnings of any fires or enemy armies approaching. At night a fire was lit on top of the turret to guide the citizens to their destinations. The area was badly bombed during the Second World War and is now being extensively redeveloped.

Bartholomew Fair Held in the churchyard of the Priory of St Bartholomew, Smithfield [2D 61b], every third week in August from 1133 until 1855; this is the longest record for any fair held in England. Cloth Fair [2D 61b] and Hosier Lane [2C 61a], Smithfield, are reminders that clothiers from all over England and drapers from London frequented the fair. The few stalls in nearby Farringdon Road [1B 61a] are all that remains of Bartholomew Fair.

Bateman Street, Soho [3D 60d] Commemorates the name of Lord Bateman who bought Monmouth House after the death in 1685 of the Duke of Monmouth; the mansion stood near or on the site of the Soho Hospital for Women, Soho Square. It was said of his lordship that although the king made him a lord, he could not make him a gentleman.

Battersea Park [2B 76] Laid out by Thomas Cubitt (*see main entry*) on the site of the Battersea Fields and opened to the public in 1859. The Festival

Gardens, opened in 1951 as part of the Festival of Britain, contain a funfair. Battersea derives its name from either Peters-Ey or Patricks-Ey; Ey meaning Island. The name describes the area as being a piece of land bordering on an island belonging to the Abbey of St Peter at Westminster.

Bayswater [2A 60a] Land that belonged to Bairnardus of Normandy, thought to be an officer in the service of William the Conqueror; the water supply which fed the manor house was called Baynard's Watering—hence the name Bayswater.

Bazaar In 1816 Queen Charlotte opened the Soho Bazaar, which stood on the north-west side of SOHO SQUARE [2D 60c] and was the first bazaar in Britain. It was originally built for the sale of articles to help the relatives of those killed in the Napoleonic Wars. As the government opposed the proposal the bazaar was opened with private money.

Beaufort, Sir Francis (1774-1857) Admiral and hydrographer, who invented the Beaufort Scale, a method of indicating the speed of wind. He lived at 51 MANCHESTER STREET, Baker Street, W.1. [2F 60b].

Beerbohm, Max (1872-1956) Essayist, critic and caricaturist. Born at 57 PALACE GARDENS TERRACE, Kensington [2F 59]. His best-known works are *The Works of Max Beerbohm*, the novel *Zuleika Dobson* and *The Poet's Corner*. In 1956 his ashes were brought back from Rapallo in Italy, where he had lived since 1910, for burial in ST PAUL'S CATHEDRAL.

Belfry Club, 13 West Halkin Street, Belgrave Square [2F 62B] Looks like a church. It was built in 1830 as a daughter church to St Columba's, Pont Street, and rebuilt in 1882 as the Belgrave Presbyterian Church.

In 1923 a Mrs Maund bought the lease and converted it into a private house, and in 1945 it was acquired by a Miss Lane who founded the Belfry Club.

Belgians' Memorial Erected on the VICTORIA EMBANKMENT [1E 62d] in 1920. It commemorates the hospitality of the people of Britain to Belgians during the First World War. When Princess Charlotte died in childbirth, her husband, Prince Leopold, continued to live in Marlborough House until 1831, when he returned to Belgium to be its first king.

Belgrave Square, Belgravia [2F 62b] Laid out by Thomas Cubitt (*see main entry*) in 1828 to George Basevi's designs in an area known as the Five Fields. The name 'Belgrave' comes from a village in Leicestershire, where the Grosvenor family had one of its many estates. These fields, a clayey swamp, were much frequented by duellists, footpads and vagabonds.

Belsize Park, Swiss Cottage [2A 44] Occupies part of the site of the manor of Belsize, which was granted to Westminster Abbey by Edward II. In 1720 the manor was converted into a place of entertainment, which apparently sank into low repute. It was later reconverted into a private residence. When the manor was demolished in 1852 the bricks were reused for building the roads that now cover the Belsize estate.

Berlioz, Hector [1803-69] French composer. His works include the *Symphonie Fantastique*, *La Damnation de Faust* and the opera *The Trojans*. His memoirs were translated into English. He lived for a time at 58 QUEEN ANNE STREET, Wimpole Street [2A 60c].

Bermondsey Known as leather land, because it was the centre of the leather trade for almost 300 years.

Part of it is also occupied by docks. Every Friday in Bermondsey Square [2A 63c] a market (transferred from the Caledonian Market, Islington) takes place.

Bethnal Green Now incorporated in the Borough of Tower Hamlets, but originally a hamlet in the parish of Stepney. Its name is a contraction of Bathon Hall, the residence of the Bathon family, who lived here at the end of the thirteenth century. BETHNAL GREEN MUSEUM in CAMBRIDGE HEATH ROAD [1E 61d] opened in June 1872. It was established with some of the exhibits from the Hyde Park Exhibition of 1851, which the government offered to all London districts; however, Bethnal Green was the only one to apply.

Betterton Street, Drury Lane [2E 60d] Named after Thomas Betterton (1637-1710), actor. His father was an undercook to Charles I. He himself was apprenticed to a bookseller, but turned actor and in 1695 became a partner of a theatre that was opened in LINCOLN'S INN FIELDS; as an actor he was acclaimed as a genius. He is buried in the cloisters of WESTMINSTER ABBEY.

Bible Translator Miles Coverdale (1488-1568) was in 1548 appointed chaplain to Edward VI and three years later was created Bishop of London. His translation of the Bible, which appeared in 1535, was the first complete version to be printed in English. He was rector from 1564 to 1566 at ST MAGNUS THE MARTYR, MONUMENT, E.C.3. [4F 61b], where he is buried.

Big Ben The bell attached to the clock on the Clock Tower of the HOUSES OF PARLIAMENT (*see main entry*). Named after Sir Benjamin Hall, first Commissioner of Works. The first bell was cast in 1856 near Stockton-on-Tees, but within a few months, it had to be removed and broken down because of

The clock tower of the Houses of Parliament. This tower is often thought of, and referred to, as Big Ben. In fact, the name should apply only to its largest bell, which can be heard chiming on every hour.

defective casting. The second and present one was cast in 1858 in Messrs Mears Foundry in Whitechapel Road, E.1. Besides the big bell, which weighs nearly fourteen tons, there are four small bells on which the quarter-hours chime.

Big Benzine The dial of the clock on top of Shell Mex House overlooking the VICTORIA EMBANKMENT [1E 62d] is 25 ft 3 in in diameter compared with Big Ben's 23 ft. It is the largest clock face in the country and known facetiously as Big Benzine.

Billingsgate Market [4F 61b] London's premier fish market is the oldest market owned by the City Corporation. Billingsgate may have got its name from an ancient British king named Belin, or from a Roman settler named Belinus. An act of Parliament in 1699 made Billingsgate a free and open market for the sale of fish, which meant that the fishmongers who purchased fish here had the right to resell it anywhere. Another Act (in 1846) enacted that the market be open six days a week for the wholesale and retail sale of fish.

Birdcage Walk [2C 62c] On the south side of St James's Park. It derives its name from the aviary in which Charles II caged a variety of birds. Extending from BIRDCAGE WALK to QUEEN ANNE'S GATE are COCKPIT STEPS, which led to a pit where cock-fighting took place. The pit was removed in 1816 but the steps remain.

Birth Control Dr Marie Stopes (1880-1958), scientist and writer, was the first woman to be appointed to the science staff at Manchester University in 1904. Author of *Married Love* and *Radiant Motherhood.* In 1921 she founded the country's first birth-control clinic in HOLLOWAY; four years later it moved to its present quarters at 108 WHITFIELD STREET, Tottenham Court Road.

Bishopsgate [2A 61c] This gate is thought to have been built in about 685 by one of the Bishops of London. It stood just south of St Botolph's churchyard, between WORMWOOD STREET and CAMOMILE STREET, Bishopsgate. It was demolished in 1761. In Roman times the main road leading north out of London passed this point.

Bishop's Way, Hackney Road [3F 47] Built on land known as Bishop Bonner's Fields; this was the property of Edmund Bonner (1500-69), a favourite of Henry VIII, who was appointed Bishop of London in 1539. Edward VI confined him to the Marshalsea

Prison, but he gained favour with Queen Mary, who restored his bishopric. Refusing to accept the supremacy of Elizabeth I, he was again confined to Marshalsea, where he died.

Blackfriars [4C 61a] Derives its name from the monastery of Dominicans or Black Friars, established by the Earl of Kent in 1221.

Blackfriars Bridge [4C 61a] The first bridge was opened in November 1769 and demolished in 1863. The second and present one was opened by Queen Victoria on 6 November 1869. This was the first London bridgehead to have an underpass, which was opened in July 1967.

Blackheath [3E 81] An open common once noted for its highwaymen. It is thought to have derived its name from its misty position. Here Wat Tyler in 1381 and Jack Cabe in 1450 set up their headquarters before they marched on to London. At SHOOTERS HILL, off Blackheath [3E 81], archery used to be practised.

Blake, William (1757-1827) Poet and painter. Born in BROADWICK STREET, Soho [3C 60c]. He studied at the Royal Academy. His best-known poems are probably 'The Tiger', 'The Lamb' and 'Jerusalem', and many of his pictures can be seen in the Tate Gallery (*see main entry*). He lived at 17 SOUTH MOLTON STREET, Oxford Street [3A 60c], and in a house in HERCULES ROAD, Lambeth [3A 63a], where Blake House now stands. Buried in BUNHILL FIELDS, Moorgate.

Bligh, William (1754-1817) Admiral. In 1772 he sailed round the world with Captain Cook. In 1787 he was appointed commander of the *Bounty*. Because of his harsh treatment his crew mutinied and set him adrift with eighteen men, but he was rescued and later appointed Governor of New South Wales, Australia. His opposition to the civil and military authorities there earned him a two-year prison sentence and he was expelled to England. He lived at 100 LAMBETH ROAD [3F 62d] and is buried at ST MARY'S, LAMBETH.

Blondin, Charles (1824-97) French-born acrobat and tightrope walker, whose real name was Jean François Gravelet. He crossed the Niagara Falls on his tightrope over 300 times, and in 1862 at the Crystal Palace he performed at a height of 170 ft from the ground. He named his residence in NORTHFIELD AVENUE, Ealing [2A 56], Niagara House, and the adjacent BLONDIN AVENUE commemorates his name. He is buried in KENSAL GREEN CEMETERY.

Blood Circulation William Harvey (1578-1657), author of *Exercitationes De Generatione Animalium*, was physician to Charles I and chief physician at BART'S HOSPITAL (*see Hospital*) 1609-43. It was in this hospital that he discovered the circulation of blood; his theory was published in 1628.

Bloody Bridge The bridge that led from CLIVEDEN PLACE [3F 62b] to the king's private road (now part of the KING'S ROAD, Chelsea) was, according to a map of 1775 and to a letter from Sir Hans Sloane to the Lords Commissioners, called the Bloody Bridge. It probably got its name because this area was part of the Five Fields, which were infested with highwaymen and vagabonds.

Bluecoat School, Christ's Hospital Founded by Edward VI in 1552 as a hospital for foundlings and poor fatherless children. This establishment stood almost opposite the OLD BAILEY in NEWGATE STREET, City, on the site of the Grey Friars Monastery. From the uniform worn by the boys, it later became known as the Bluecoat School. In 1902 the school moved to its present quarters in Horsham, Sussex.

Blue Lamp Stewarts Licensed Taxi Garage, which came to its present quarters in Farm Lane, near the FULHAM BROADWAY [2F 75], in June 1970 is known to the cab trade as 'The Blue Lamp', because a number of its drivers are ex-policemen.

Blunder Pass London's first underpass, at HYDE PARK CORNER [3C 60], was opened by the Duke of Wellington on 17 October 1962. This project was sponsored by Mr Ernest Marples, then Minister of Transport, and cost nearly £6,000,000 to build. It was called the Blunder Pass, because at each end of the tunnel four lines of traffic converge into three.

The monument to Queen Boadicea.

Boadicea 'Queen of the Iceni in the east of Britain' led a revolt against the Romans. In AD 61, after being defeated by the invaders, she poisoned her daughter and then herself. Legend has it that she was routed at Battle Bridge – hence BATTLE BRIDGE ROAD [3F 45] – King's Cross, and buried where King's Cross Station now stands. Monument at the junction of VICTORIA EMBANKMENT and WESTMINSTER BRIDGE [1E 62d].

Boat Race The first boat race between Oxford and Cambridge was held at Henley in 1829 and the race has been rowed annually at about Eastertime since 1856. It starts at Putney Bridge and finishes at Mortlake, a distance of just under four and a quarter miles. Only once to date – in 1877 – has the race been declared a draw.

Bolivia Simon Bolivar (1783-1830), called the Liberator, fought for freedom with the patriots of Venezuela, Colombia and Peru. Bolivia was named after him. In 1810 he came to London as the Venezuelan representative and lived at 4 DUKE STREET, Wigmore Street [3F 60b].

Bond Street Fashionable shopping street. OLD BOND STREET [4B 60c] was built in 1686 by Sir Thomas Bond of Hill Street, Peckham, Comptroller to the Royal Household of the Queen Mother, Henrietta Maria. NEW BOND STREET [3A 60c] was built in 1721 on an open field, called the Conduit Mead after a conduit which supplied the area with water. CONDUIT STREET [3B 60c] extends from New Bond Street to Regent Street.

Booth, Charles (1840-1916) Shipowner and research worker. He investigated the poverty in the East End of London, advocated old-age pensions and wrote *Life and Labour of the People in London.* He lived at 6 GRENVILLE PLACE, Cromwell Road [3A 62a].

Borrow, George (1803-81) Author and traveller. Correspondent for *The Times* and agent for the British and Foreign Bible Society in Russia and Spain. Author of *Romany Rye* and *Lavengro*. He lived from 1860 to 1874 at 22 HEREFORD SQUARE, Gloucester Road [4A 62a].

Boswell, James (1740-95) Son of a Scottish judge. In 1763 he first met Dr Johnson (*see Dictionary*), whose close friend and biographer he became; his best-known work is *The Life of Dr Johnson*. He lived and died in a house on the site of 120 GREAT PORTLAND STREET, Oxford Street, Kensington [1B 60c].

Botany Bay In about 1851 the area round BONNER ROAD, Hackney [4F 47], was demolished to build Victoria Park and the City of London Hospital for Diseases of the Chest. It was formerly known as Botany Bay, because so many of the local residents were sent to the penal settlement of that name in Australia.

Botolph Lane, Eastcheap [4F 61b] Commemorates Botolph (died 680), an English Benedictine monk who founded a monastery that was destroyed by the Danes. Many churches, including the ones at Aldersgate, Bishopsgate and Aldgate, are dedicated to this saint.

Bottled Beer Alexander Nowell (1507-1602), headmaster of Westminster School 1543-55 and Dean of St Paul's Cathedral from 1560 until his death, is credited with accidently inventing bottled beer. It appears that he went fishing at Battersea Fields (where BATTERSEA PARK – *see main entry* – now is), then private property, and unwittingly left a bottle of ale when chased out of the fields. On his return a few days later, he was amazed to discover the contents of the bottle in prime condition.

Bow Now incorporated into the Borough of Tower Hamlets. It is said to have taken its name from an arched (bow) bridge that spanned the River Lea. The Bridge, which was replaced in 1839, was built by Queen Matilda, wife of Henry I, after she had had a narrow escape from drowning.

Bowler Hats The first bowler hat was reputedly made in 1810 by Lock's the hatters of 6 ST JAMES'S STREET, Piccadilly [4B 60c], to the order of a Mr Coke, who wanted to wear it at a hunt at Holkham Hall in Norfolk. The hats were originally known as billycocks.

Bow Street, Covent Garden [2E 49] So called because it is shaped like a bent bow. The street is famed for the ROYAL OPERA HOUSE and for BOW STREET POLICE COURT, the chief of the metropolitan police courts, built in 1881 (*see also Police Station Lights*). The first courthouse opened there in 1748 and the Bow Street Runners (*see Mobile Police*) were predecessors of the modern police.

Box Office In the sixteenth century it was the custom for a trumpet to be blown outside places of entertainment just before the play started. The audience would then enter and pay their entrance fee. This money was collected in locked boxes and given to the management – hence the term 'box office'.

Boy Scouts Movement founded in 1908 by Sir Robert, later Lord, Baden-Powell (1857-1941), who saw active service in India and Mafeking. The first Boy Scout Rally was held at the CRYSTAL PALACE on 4 September 1909, when the scouts paraded before the founder. Statue outside BADEN-POWELL HOUSE, QUEEN'S GATE, South Kensington [2A 62a].

Bridewell Prison Stood on or near 14 NEW BRIDGE

STREET, Ludgate Circus [3C 61a], on the site of a royal palace and near the Well of St Bride. Edward VI converted the palace into a hospital and later ceded it to the City Corporation, who, in turn, converted it into a house of correction. The prison was rebuilt after being partly destroyed in the Great Fire of 1666 but was demolished in 1863.

Bridges There are eighteen road bridges and nine railway bridges over the Thames between the sea and Teddington. The first stone bridge was the original LONDON BRIDGE (*see main entry*), built between 1176 and 1209. TOWER BRIDGE (*see main entry*), built 1886-94, is the last bridge on the way down to the sea. ALBERT BRIDGE, built in 1873, is a combined cantilever and suspension Bridge designed by R. M. Ordish.

Albert Bridge.

The British Museum, viewed from its gates.

British Museum, Great Russell Street [2D 60d] The museum is the largest of its kind in the world. It was founded in 1753. In 1755 Montague House, which stood on the site of the present museum, was purchased after a public lottery. Soon more space was needed for the growing collections, so the existing buildings were designed by Robert and Sidney Smirke and built between 1823 and 1847. The British Museum is the national museum of archaeology and ethnography; its most famous exhibits are the Rosetta Stone (*see main entry*) and the Elgin Marbles, taken from the Parthenon in Athens. The library contains over six million volumes and receives a copy of every work published in Britain.

Brompton Hospital, Fulham Road [4B 62a] Originally established in 1841 at the Chelsea Manor House, the hospital now occupies the site of the Botanical Gardens founded by William Curtis (d. 1799), the entomologist. Its present quarters were built by the founder, Philip Rose, a solicitor. The hospital's full title was the Brompton Hospital for Consumption and Diseases of the Chest and it was built at a time when nearly 60,000 people a year died from consumption, and the expectation of life for the average workman was about seventeen years.

Brooks's Club Founded in 1764 by the Duke of Portland and Charles James Fox, the club has been at its present quarters in ST JAMES'S STREET, Piccadilly [4B 60c], since 1788. Brooks's Club is noted for the fact that its members' horses have won the Derby on at least fifty occasions. There is a cockpit under its boiler-room.

Brook Street, Mayfair [3A 60c] Built on the site of a cattle market known as Brook Field, which in turn took its name from the brook that once came down from Tyburn and flowed across Piccadilly.

Brougham Bridge Brougham, Lord Henry Peter (1778-1868) Lawyer and statesman, Member of Parliament 1810-12 and 1816-30, and one of the founders of University College, London. He invented the carriage named after him. In 1894 he introduced the game of bridge to this country. He lived the last thirty years of his life at 4 GRAFTON STREET, New Bond Street [3A 60c].

Browning, Elizabeth Barrett (1806-61) Poet. An invalid from the age of fifteen, she lived at 99 GLOUCESTER PLACE, Baker Street [1E 60b], and 1838-46 at 50 WIMPOLE STREET [2A 60c], where she met Robert Browning. She married the poet secretly at the old Marylebone parish church in 1846 and they went to live in Venice, where she died. Her best poems are *Sonnets from the Portuguese*.

Browning, Robert (1812-89) Poet. Born in SOUTHAMPTON WAY, Camberwell [2C 78], and studied at University College, London. After the death in Venice in 1861 of his wife, Elizabeth Barrett Browning, he moved in 1862 to 19 WARWICK CRESCENT, Maida Vale [1A 60a], ('Little Venice'), because it reminded him of Venice. He lived there until 1887, then from 1887 to his death at 29 DE VERE GARDENS, Kensington [3F 59]. His poems include 'The Pied Piper of Hamelin', 'Home Thoughts from Abroad' and 'My Last Duchess'. He is buried in Poet's Corner, WESTMINSTER ABBEY.

Brunel, Father and Son Isambard Kingdom Brunel (1806-59), civil engineer, was in 1833 appointed engineer to the Great Western Railway. He designed the *Great Britain*, which was the first ocean-going screw-propeller steamship, and erected the docks at Brentford, Bristol and Plymouth. He lived with his father, Sir Marc Isambard Brunel (1769-1849), inventor, engineer and builder of ROTHERHITHE TUNNEL (*see main entry*), at 98 CHEYNE WALK, Chelsea [1A 76]. The son's statue is on VICTORIA EMBANKMENT [1E 62d]. BRUNEL ROAD, Rotherhithe Tunnel [2F 63d] commemorates the father.

Buckingham Palace. The flying standard indicates that the Sovereign is in residence.

Buckingham Palace [2B 60c] Built in 1703 by John Sheffield, Duke of Buckingham, who named it Buckingham House. Bought by George III in 1762 and rebuilt by Nash between 1825 and 1836. After Queen Victoria's accession in 1837 it became the permanent London residence of the sovereign. The façade was redesigned in 1913 by Sir Aston Webb. The interior is never open to the public, but the QUEEN'S GALLERY (entered from Buckingham Palace Road) puts on exhibitions of items drawn from the royal collection.

Buckland, Francis Trevelyan (1826-80) Naturalist. He studied medicine at St George's Hospital, Hyde Park Corner, where he was house surgeon for a short time. An expert on the artificial rearing of salmon, he was appointed inspector of salmon fisheries in 1867. Author of *Fish-hatching* and *Curiosities of Natural History*. He lived and died at 37 ALBANY STREET, Regent's Park [3D 45].

Bunhill Fields, Moorgate [2E 61b] The name comes from 'bone-hill'. In 1549 many bodies taken from the old St Paul's were reburied here. After the Plague of 1665, it was used as a plague pit, but an Act of Parliament in 1867 prohibited further burials. The mother of John Wesley (*see Methodist*), Daniel Defoe, John Bunyan, Isaac Watts and William Blake (*see main entries*) are buried in the Fields, which were the principal burial place for Nonconformists from 1685.

Bunyan, John (1628-88) Author. He worked as a tinker and later fought against Charles I in the Civil War. In 1660 he was sent to prison for twelve years for preaching for the Nonconformist Church without a licence, and later served a shorter sentence. He is best known for *The Pilgrim's Progress*. Statue on the Baptist Church, SOUTHAMPTON ROW, Kingsway [1E 60d]. Buried in BUNHILL FIELDS, Moorgate.

Burdett Road, Bow [1B 64] Named in honour of Baroness Burdett-Coutts (1814-1906), who was instrumental in founding the National Society for the Prevention of Cruelty to Children and the Royal Society for the Prevention of Cruelty to Animals. She was the first woman to receive the freedom of the City of London, was created a baroness in 1871 and is buried in WESTMINSTER ABBEY.

'Burglars' Avenue' THE BISHOPS AVENUE [2B 28], a very select residential area off Hampstead Lane, N.2., is often called 'Millionaires' Avenue', but at one time, because of the numerous robberies that had taken place there, the residents called it 'Burglars' Avenue'.

Burgoyne, John (1722-92) Soldier and dramatist, called 'Gentleman Johnny'. He entered Parliament in 1768. He commanded the British troops in the American War of Independence, but capitulated to the Americans at Saratoga in 1777. After the war he wrote comedies such as *The Lord of the Manor* and *The Heiress*. He lived at 10 HERTFORD STREET, Mayfair [1A 62c]. Buried in WESTMINSTER ABBEY.

Burke, Edmund (1729-97) Irish-born author and Whig Member of Parliament. Modern Conservatives regard him as one of their great political theorists. His writings include *A Vindication of Natural Society* and *Reflections on the Revolution in France*. He lived at 37 GERRARD STREET, Shaftesbury Avenue [3D 60d].

Burne-Jones, Sir Edward (1833-98) Pre-Raphaelite designer and painter. His paintings include 'The Golden Stairs' and 'King Cophetua and the Begger Maid'. He lived 1856-9 at 17 RED LION SQUARE, Holborn [2F 60d].

Burney, Fanny (1752-1840) Novelist and diarist. In

1786 she was appointed Second Keeper of the Robes to Queen Charlotte. Seven years later, she married General D'Arblay, a French refugee, and spent most of her married life in France, where she was interned by Napoleon. Her best known work is *Evelina.* She lived at 11 BOLTON STREET, Piccadilly [4B 60c].

Burns, Robert (1759-96) Scottish poet and farmer. He is best known for his songs 'Auld Lang Syne' and 'Ye Banks and Braes o' Bonny Doon' and for his poems 'To a Mouse' and 'My Love is like a Red Red Rose'. Monument in the gardens of VICTORIA EMBANKMENT [4F 60d].

Buxton Memorial, Victoria Tower Gardens [3E 62d] This monument, which formerly stood at the junction of GREAT GEORGE STREET and PARLIAMENT SQUARE, was designed and built in 1865 by Mr C. Buxton, MP, as a memorial to those Members of Parliament who advocated the abolition of the slave trade.

Byron, Lord George (1788-1824) Poet. Born in HOLLES STREET, Oxford Street [2B 60c] and baptized at the old Marlyebone parish church. His best-known works are 'Childe Harold' and 'Don Juan'. In 1823 he went to Greece to help in the struggle for independence against the Turks and died of fever. He lived at 8 ST JAMES'S STREET, Piccadilly [4B 60c], where Byron House now stands. There is also a statue of him on South East Corner in Hyde Park [1F 62b].

C

Cabmen's Maze, Pimlico [4C 62c] Pimlico may have taken its name from Ben Pimlico, an inn-keeper, or from The Pimlico, a tavern that stood in Buckingham Palace Road, or from a kind of drink. Because of its many intricate streets, made worse by its one-way system, it is popularly known as the Cabmen's Maze.

Cabmen's Shelters In February 1875 the Hon. A. Kinnaird, MP, opened London's first cab shelter in Acacia Road, St John's Wood [3B 44]. The cabmen's shelter in the centre of the road by the Brompton Oratory [3C 62a] is called The Bell and Horns, and took its name from a tavern that once stood in Brompton Road.

Camden Town The Borough of Camden includes Hampstead, Holborn and St Pancras. Camden Town [3D-E 45] was built between 1791 and 1804 and named after Lord Camden (1714-94), the ground landlord, Member of Parliament, Attorney General and Chief Justice of the Court of Common Pleas, who was appointed Lord Chancellor in 1765.

Campbell, Mrs Patrick (1865-1940) English actress. She came to fame in 1893 with her performance in Pinero's *The Second Mrs Tanqueray*. She was renowned for her portrayal of such characters as Juliet in *Romeo and Juliet* and Eliza Doolittle in *Pygmalion* by George Bernard Shaw (*see main entry*), of whom she was a close friend. She lived at 33 Kensington Square,

High Street Kensington [3F 59].

Canada Walk [2F 60d] To commemorate the headquarters of the Royal Canadian Air Force which was housed in LINCOLN'S INN FIELDS (*see main entry*) 1940-5 Holborn Borough Council named the north side of the Fields 'Canada Walk'.

Canaletto, Antonio (1697-1768) Venetian painter noted for his paintings of his own city. He visited England from 1746 until about 1756 and painted a number of English views. His paintings include *View on the Grand Canal* and *Eton College*. He lived 1749-51 at 41 BEAK STREET, Regent Street [3C 60c].

Candles In 1830 Price's Patent Candle Company, one of the largest candle producers in the country, began as a partnership in Vauxhall. Thirty years later it moved to its present quarters in YORK ROAD, Battersea [3A 76]. The factory was built on the site of York House, a manor thought to have been erected in about 1475 by Lawrence Booth, Bishop of Durham, who later presented the house to the Archbishops of York.

Canning, George (1770-1827) Born in London of Irish parents, but orphaned when young. He entered Parliament in 1793 and was foreign secretary 1807-9 and 1822-7. He supported the movement for Greek independence. He was prime minister from February 1827 until his death in August of the same year. He lived at 37 CONDUIT STREET, New Bond Street [3B 60c], and died in CHISWICK HOUSE (*see main entry*). Statue in PARLIAMENT SQUARE.

Cannon Street, City [3D 61b] Rebuilt and extended to St Paul's Cathedral in 1854. Originally called Candlewick Street, from the candle-makers who had lived there earlier and made candles for the Roman Catholic Church. Its construction was opposed by the city traders who claimed it would not relieve the traffic congestion prevailing in those days.

Canonbury, Islington The name is presumed to come from the Priory of the Canons of St Bartholomew in the City; the priors had a country residence here from the end of the eleventh century. It was on the site of this mansion that CANONBURY PLACE [2B 46] was built.

Caribee Islands This was a maze of passages and alleyways, near ST MARTIN-IN-THE-FIELDS, TRAFALGAR SQUARE. A haven for rogues and vagabonds, it was demolished in 1829, to make way for CHANDOS STREET [2B 60c].

Carmelite Street, Victoria Embankment [3B 61a] Derives its name from the Carmelites, a monastic order of friars originally from Mount Carmel. In 1241 they built a priory on the site of present-day CARMELITE and WHITEFRIARS STREETS. The latter street derives its name from the habit worn by the friars.

Car Park Europe's largest underground car park, in East Carriage Road, HYDE PARK, was opened on 15 October 1962, by Harold Macmillan, then prime minister. It is often called the 'Cemetery' by its patrons.

Carlton, Poor One of London's leading hotels, erected in 1899 on the present site of New Zealand House, Haymarket. Badly bombed in 1940. Demolished in 1948. Bruce House, a large working man's hostel built in 1906 by the London County Council (still standing), is often called 'The Poor Man's Carlton.'

Carlton House Built in 1709 for Lord Carlton and

from 1783 the home of George IV when he was Prince of Wales, the mansion was demolished in 1826. The Duke of York's Column now stands on the site. CARLTON HOUSE TERRACE [1D 62d] was built in 1827.

Carlyle, Thomas (1795-1881) Scottish-born essayist, historian, lecturer and biographer; his works include *The French Revolution*, *Sartor Resartus* and *History of Frederick the Great*. He lived from 1834 till his death at 24 CHEYNE ROW, Chelsea [1B 76]. This house, known as Carlyle's House, is now a National Trust House. There is also a statue in the gardens in CHEYNE WALK. (*See also Soundproof*.)

Carnaby Street, Soho [3C 60c] The symbol of the 'Swinging London' of the 1960s, the street is famous for its boutiques. It is now for the use of pedestrians only.

Thomas Carlyle, Scottish-born essayist, historian, lecturer and biographer.

Caslon, William (1692-1766) England's first great typefounder. His foundry was erected in 1737 on the site of 21 CHISWELL STREET, Moorgate [1E 61b] and demolished in 1909. He is buried in ST LUKE'S, OLD STREET, City [4C 46]. CASLON STREET, adjacent to the church, commemorates his name.

Cathedral Prison On the site of WESTMINSTER CATHEDRAL (*see main entry*) stood Tothill Prison, the Westminster House of Correction, erected in 1618. After the defeat of Charles II at Worcester in 1651 the Scottish prisoners taken by Cromwell were interned here. It was rebuilt in 1826 and demolished in 1884.

Cato Street Conspirators In 1820 a number of men under the leadership of a Mr Thistlewood met in a loft in CATO STREET [2D 60b], off Harrowby Street, Edgware Road, and plotted to murder the entire Cabinet at a dinner given by Lord Harrowby. On information received, the Bow Street Runners raided the loft. One policeman was killed and three were wounded. On 11 May the same year six of the conspirators, including Mr Thistlewood, were hanged at NEWGATE PRISON.

Cavell, Edith Louisa (1865-1915) Nurse, daughter of a vicar. She trained as a nurse at the LONDON HOSPITAL, WHITECHAPEL ROAD, and became matron of a medical institute in Brussels that became a Red Cross hospital during the First World War. During the German occupation she harboured wounded soldiers and refugees, helping them to escape. Arrested and court-martialled by the Germans, she was shot on 12 October 1915. There is a monument to her in CHARING CROSS ROAD, near Trafalgar Square [3D 60d]. CAVELL STREET, behind the London Hospital [2E 61d], commemorates her name.

Cavendish Square, Oxford Street [2A 60c] Constructed in 1717 for Edward Harley, later second Earl of Oxford. He married Henrietta Cavendish Holles, daughter of the Duke of Newcastle who had bought the manor of Marylebone in 1710. Their daughter, Margaret, married the Duke of Portland. The names of these families and of their estates are remembered in the street names in this area—Bentinck, Cavendish, Devonshire, Harley, Henrietta, Holles, Margaret, Portland, Wigmore, Wimpole, Weymouth. (*See also Great Titchfield Street.*)

Caxton, William (1422-91) First English printer. He learned printing in Cologne and set up his own press in Bruges. In 1476 he set up the first printing press in England on a site close to WESTMINSTER ABBEY. In 1482 he acquired larger premises in the Almonry which stood at what is now the junction of VICTORIA STREET and GREAT SMITH STREET [2D 62d]. He printed about 100 books, many of them translations by himself of French romances. He is buried in ST MARGARET'S, WESTMINSTER (*see Parliament's Church*).

Cayley, Sir George (1774-1857) Pioneer of aviation, Member of Parliament, scientist, inventor of the bicycle wheel, fountain pen, caterpillar tractor, a self righting lifeboat and artificial limbs. He lived at 20 HERTFORD STREET, Mayfair [1A 62c].

Cenotaph The name means an empty tomb. The Cenotaph, erected in WHITEHALL [1E 62d] in memory of those who fell in the First World War, was unveiled by King George V on 11 November 1920. Designed by Sir Edwin Lutyens, who lived at 13 MANSFIELD STREET, Portland Place [2A 60c].

Chalk Farm Derives its name from Chalcot Farm which stood on the site of ENGLANDS LANE and

CHALCOT GARDENS [2C 44] and was once a favourite meeting-place for duellists. In 1821, John Scott, editor of the *London Magazine*, was killed here in one of the last duels to take place in England. His opponent, Mr Christik, was tried for murder at the Old Bailey but acquitted.

Chamberlain, Joseph (1836-1914) Statesman, father of Neville Chamberlain. Born at 188 CAMBERWELL GROVE, Camberwell Green (3C 78]. He did much for the development of Birmingham where he was three times mayor. Later he represented the city in Parliament. He was president of the Board of Trade and twice colonial secretary. He lived 1845-54 at 25 HIGHBURY PLACE, Highbury Corner [2B 46] and died at 40 PRINCES GARDENS, Kensington [2B 62a].

Chamberlain, Neville (1869-1940) Conservative statesman, known as the 'Appeaser'. He became prime minister in 1937 and in 1938 flew twice to Germany to meet Hitler with his 'peace at any price' policy. He died within a few months of his resignation in 1940. He lived 1923-35 at 37 EATON SQUARE, Belgravia [3F 62b]. Buried in WESTMINSTER ABBEY.

Chancery Lane, Fleet Street [2A 61a] Originally called Chancellor's Lane. From 1232 until 1377, a Carthusian house stood on the site of the present PUBLIC RECORD OFFICE; it was built by Henry III (r. 1216-72) for use by converted Jews who lived there under a guidance of a Christian governor. The Public Record Office houses the national archives and a small museum (*see also Domesday Book*).

Changing of the Guard One of the most popular tourist spectacles in London. The ceremony of the changing of the Queen's Guard takes place daily at BUCKINGHAM PALACE at 11.30 a.m. The changing of the Queen's Life Guard takes place in the small courtyard of the Horse Guards in WHITEHALL at 11 am (10 am on Sundays).

Chapels The cab-ranks in WHITECHAPEL ROAD, at the junction of Leman Street [3C 61c], and at ST JOHN'S WOOD roundabout, opposite St John's Wood Church (4B 44), are referred to as 'Chapels'.

Charing Cross (4E 60d] To mark the resting places of the body of his wife, Queen Eleanor, on her last journey from Harby in Nottinghamshire to Westminster Abbey for burial, King Edward I erected twelve crosses as memorials. The last one was in the village of Charing. The monument was destroyed by Cromwell's Puritans in 1647, and the copy that stands in the courtyard of Charing Cross Station was erected in 1863. (*See also Cheapside Cross.*)

Charles I (1600-49) He became king in 1625 and from 1629-40 ruled without a parliament. Civil war broke out in 1642 and three years later he was defeated at Naseby by Cromwell's Roundheads. He was executed before the BANQUETING HOUSE in WHITEHALL opposite the Horse Guards [1E 62d]. Statue in TRAFALGAR SQUARE.

Charles II (1630-85) Son of Charles I, he came to the throne after the death of Cromwell in 1660. He formed a liaison with Nell Gwyn, and was known as the merry monarch. Outstanding events during his reign were the Plague of 1665, the Great Fire of 1666 and the Habeas Corpus Act of 1679. He died in WHITEHALL PALACE, Whitehall [1E 62d], and is buried in WESTMINSTER ABBEY. Statue in SOHO SQUARE [2D 60d].

'Charlies' Before 1830 night-watchmen were called

Charlies, allegedly after Charles I. In May of that year an Act of Parliament created the Night Police of the Metropolis, in which many of the Charlies enlisted.

Charterhouse [1C 61a] In 1371, Sir Walter De Manny founded in Charterhouse Square, Smithfield, a monastery for the Carthusian monks, whose name of Chartreuse, (where they were founded in France), became corrupted into Charterhouse. In 1611, it was bought by Thomas Sutton, a colliery owner, who converted it to a school and a home for the aged poor. The School, Charterhouse, removed in 1882 to Godalming, in Surrey, and then the Merchant Taylor's School took over until 1933.

Chatham House, 10 St James's Square [46 60c] The home of Pitt the Elder (*see main entry*) 1759-62, of the fourteenth Earl of Derby 1837-55, and of Mr Gladstone (*see main entry*) in 1890, all three of them prime ministers. It now houses the Royal Institute of International Affairs.

Chaucer, Geoffrey (1340-1400) Poet. He also held various court and official positions in the king's service. His works include *The House of Fame*, *Troilus and Criseyde* and the famous *Canterbury Tales*. He lived in LEADENHALL STREET, near Aldgate Pump [3A 61c], and was the first poet to be buried in Poets' Corner, WESTMINSTER ABBEY.

Cheapside, City [3D-E 61b] Takes its name from the Anglo-Saxon word '*ceap*' – to bargain or sell. BREAD STREET, IRONMONGER LANE, MILK STREET and POULTRY all bear the names of the commodities sold in the streets that lead out of Cheapside.

Cheapside Cross Stood in the centre of the road in CHEAPSIDE facing Wood Street [3D 61b]. Erected in 1290 and demolished in May 1643, this was one of the twelve crosses erected by Edward I to mark the resting places of the body of Queen Eleanor (*see also Charing Cross*).

Chelsea Incorporated the Borough of Kensington. It is said to derive its name from the word 'Chesil-Sea', meaning a shelf of sand by the water, or 'Ceal-chythe', meaning a chalk wharf.

Chelsea Arts Club Founded in 1891 by a number of artists, including J. M. Whistler (*see main entry*), at 181 KING'S ROAD [1B 76], it moved to its present quarters at 143 OLD CHURCH STREET [1B 76] in 1901. The Chelsea Arts Ball, normally held on New Year's Eve, was held annually at the ROYAL ALBERT HALL from 1908-58.

Chelsea Royal Hospital, Royal Hospital Road [1C 76] On the site of an unsuccessful theological college founded in 1609 by James I. Charles II in 1682 founded an institution for old and disabled soldiers The Hospital was built by Sir Christopher Wren 1689-90. The inmates are known as Chelsea Pensioners. The Hospital was bombed in 1918, and again in 1940 and 1945.

Chesterfield Gardens, Curzon Street, Mayfair [4A 60c] Built on the gardens of Chesterfield House. This mansion was erected in 1747 by Philip Dormer Stanhope, fourth Earl of Chesterfield (1694-1773). Writer, Member of Parliament, Ambassador to The Hague (1728) and Lord-Lieutenant of Ireland (1745). Chesterfield House, built in 1747, stood on the junction of South Audley Street, and Curzon Street, Mayfair.

Chesterton, Gilbert Keith (1874-1936) Essayist, poet, novelist. Educated at St Paul's School, Hammersmith. He invented the priest-detective Father Brown, who appears in a series of novels; his other works include *The Man Who Was Thursday* and *The Napoleon of Notting Hill.* He lived 1881-1901 at 11 WARWICK GARDENS, Kensington [4E 59].

Cheyne Walk, Chelsea [1A-B 76] In 1537 Henry VIII built a country house for Princess Elizabeth. This manor was purchased by Lord Cheyne, who, in 1708, built the road that commemorates his name. CHELSEA MANOR STREET borders on Cheyne Walk.

Chinatown Before the Second World War, certain streets around Limehouse Causeway, West India Dock Road [2B 64], contained a number of oriental restaurants and were inhabited by a number of Chinese, Japanese and Lascars, mainly seamen who were waiting for a ship. The district became popularly known as Chinatown.

Chiswick House, Burlington Lane, Chiswick [1E 73] was bought and rebuilt by the third Earl of Burlington and Cork (*d.* 1753), whose daughter married the fourth Duke of Devonshire. Queen Victoria lived at Chiswick House for a short spell, and the prime ministers Canning and Fox both died here. The house and its beautiful grounds were bought in May 1929 by the then Brentford and Chiswick Council for public use. The house was badly damaged by bombs in the Second World War, but has since been restored.

Chopin, Frederic (1810-49) Polish composer, particularly of piano music. He wrote many waltzes, preludes and nocturnes, as well as two piano concertos. From 1831 he lived in Paris. On 23 June 1848, he gave his first concert in London, where he stayed at 99 EATON PLACE, Belgravia [3F 62b].

Christmas Tree Every December since 1947 the Norwegian government has sent a Christmas tree as a gift to the people of England, in memory of the hospitality shown to the Norwegian royal family during the Second World War. The tree, which is set up in TRAFALGAR SQUARE, is illuminated free of cost.

Churchill, Sir Winston (1874-1965) Descendant of the Duke of Marlborough. He joined the Army in 1895, was war correspondent for the *Morning Post* 1899-1902 during the Boer War and entered Parliament in 1900. He married in 1908 in ST MARGARET'S CHURCH, WESTMINSTER (*see Parliament's Church*). He held various ministerial positions and became prime minister in 1940. He was thus Britain's leader in her 'finest hour' and his speeches were an inspiration both to the British people and to the allies. He lived and died at 28 HYDE PARK GATE, Kensington [2A 62a]. Monument erected in 1955 in the GUILDHALL.

Churchill's American Memorial St Mary Aldermanbury, built in about 1700 by Wren, formerly stood in LOVE LANE, off Aldermanbury in the City [2E 61b]. Damaged by bombs in the Second World War, the church was taken down stone by stone and sent to Fulton, Missouri, USA, where it was re-established as a memorial to Sir Winston Churchill. The organ, which was specially built for Woolwich Parish Church in 1741, was also sent over to Fulton in 1969. It was in a speech made at Fulton in 1946 that Churchill first used the phrase 'The Iron Curtain'. Love Lane is so called because at one time it was infested by harlots.

Cinema Licence The Biograph, WILTON ROAD,

Victoria [3B 62c], was the first cinema to be granted a cinematograph licence. Opened in 1905 as the Bioscope, it changed its name to the Biograph in 1910, the year it received its licence. The prices of admission in those days were 4d, 7d and 9d.

Citadel A solid concrete building adjoining the Admiralty in HORSEGUARDS PARADE, St James's Park [1D 62d]. It was erected in 1940 as a bomb-proof headquarters for the Admiralty, and at present is still in use as offices.

City Abbey ST HELEN'S CHURCH, Bishopsgate [2A 61c] is dedicated to the Empress Helena (d. 327), the mother of Constantine the Great. Dating from the thirteenth century, it is one of the oldest city churches. Because it contains so many monuments to famous people it is often called the 'Westminster Abbey of the City'.

City Bombs It was on FORE STREET, London Wall [2E 61b], at 12.15 am on 25 August 1940, that the first bomb fell on the City of London during the Second World War.

City Bypass EUSTON ROAD and MARYLEBONE ROAD [2D-E 60b], constructed in 1757, formed the first London bypass. Originally called the New Road, this linked Paddington with Islington and gave direct access to Essex, bypassing Oxford Street and London.

City Centres A plate on a shop at the junction of the STRAND and NORTHUMBERLAND AVENUE [4E 60d] states that the shop stands at the very centre of London, from which sign-post distances are measured. GROVELAND COURT, BOW LANE, between Watling Street and Cheapside [3E 61b], is the centre of the City of London.

City Church ST LAWRENCE JEWRY, GRESHAM STREET [2D 61b], is the official church of the City Corporation. Built on an old Jewish settlement (hence its name), it is known to have been in existence in the twelfth century. It was destroyed by the fire in 1666 and rebuilt by Sir Christopher Wren twenty years later. After being damaged by fire bombs in 1940 it was restored 1954-7. The weathervane is in the form of a gridiron, in commemoration of St Lawrence who was broiled to death on a gridiron.

City School The City of London School, established in 1834 in MILK STREET, Cheapside, moved to its present premises on the VICTORIA EMBANKMENT [3B-C 61a] in 1883. It was originally founded with land and money bequeathed by John Carpenter (1370-1441), a town clerk to the City Corporation, whose name survives in JOHN CARPENTER STREET, Victoria Embankment.

City's Festival The City of London's first festival was opened by the Lord Mayor, Sir Frederick Hoare, on 9 July 1962 and ended on 21 August. To honour the occasion, the Queen attended a show at the MANSION HOUSE, given by Billy Danvers, Tommy Steele and Randolph Sutton, and the City Corporation floodlit all its famous buildings.

City's Own The Royal Fusiliers, incorporated in the Royal Regiment of Fusiliers, is known as the City's Own because it was originally raised within the bounds of the City of London. The regiment, whose headquarters are at the TOWER OF LONDON, was awarded two Victoria Crosses in the Mons Retreat. Their memorial chapel is at ST SEPULCHRE without Newgate, Holborn Viaduct [2C 61a].

Clapham Famed for its COMMON [4D 77] upon which

many a fair has been held. It is thought to have derived its name from Clapa's Ham, the home or hamlet belonging to Osgod Clapa, the Danish war lord. The Clapham Sect was a group of prominent Anglicans, including Zachary Macaulay and William Wilberforce, which grew up in Clapham in about 1800; it fought for the abolition of slavery.

Clapham's Film For the first time in Clapham's history a world film première was held there when the film *Up the Junction* was shown at the Granada, ST JOHN'S HILL [4B 76] on 24 January 1968. Nell Dunn, the author of the book from which the film was made, attended the function; the daughter of a millionaire, she lived in Battersea for a number of years and wrote her book to describe life there.

Clarence House, Stable Yard Gate, St James's Park [1C 62c] Built in 1829 for the Duke of Clarence, who was to become William IV. It was the town residence of Princess Elizabeth before her accession to the throne in 1952, and the birthplace of Princess Anne on 15 August 1950. At present it is the home of Queen Elizabeth, the Queen Mother.

Cleopatra's Needle This granite obelisk has nothing to do with Queen Cleopatra. It was erected in Heliopolis by Thothmes III in about 1450 BC, and was later moved to Alexandria. While being brought over to England in 1878, it broke loose during a storm in the Bay of Biscay and was abandoned after six men had lost their lives. After its recovery it was erected on its present site on VICTORIA EMBANKMENT [4F 60d]. Under its foundations were buried a Bible, some coins and some newspapers of the time.

Clerkenwell [4A 46] Takes its name from the clerks' well to which the parish clerks of London came to perform their yearly miracle play. Because a great number of Italian immigrants settled here between the two world wars, it was popularly known as 'Little Italy'.

'Clink, The' This slang word for prison came from the Clink Prison that stood in or near CLINK STREET [4E 61b], near the Borough Market. This prison was built and used by the Bishops of Winchester as a place of detention for heretics. Remnants of Winchester Palace, built in the thirteenth century and occupied by the Bishops of Winchester until 1649, can still be seen from some of the enclosed warehouses.

Clive of India Baron Clive of Plassey (1725-74); soldier and statesman. He went to Madras as a writer in the East India Company in 1743 and was given an ensign's commission. He was sent to regain Calcutta in 1757 after the tragedy of the 'Black Hole'. He was appointed Governor of Bengal in 1758 and again in 1765, but resigned in 1767. Because of ill health and criticism of his conduct on Indian affairs, he committed suicide at 45 BERKELEY SQUARE [4A 60c], in the house he had bought in 1760. There is a monument on Clive Steps, Horseguards Parade, St James's Park [1E 62d].

Clown Joseph Grimaldi (1778-1837), perhaps the greatest clown of all time, started to perform at the SADLER'S WELLS THEATRE (*see main entry*), ROSEBERY AVENUE, before he was three years old. He played in pantomime at the Covent Garden and Drury Lane theatres. The many accidents he had on the stage forced him to retire in 1828. He lived and died at 22 CALSHOT STREET, Pentonville [3F 45], and was buried in the nearby churchyard (now a childrens' playground) of St James's, Pentonville Road.

Coade Lion A monumental stone lion modelled by W. F. Woodington in 1837 and made of Coade Stone. This artificial stone was once widely used, but the secret of its manufacture has been lost. The lion stood until 1949 on a parapet in front of the Lion Brewery which was demolished to make way for the Royal Festival Hall. It then stood near the exit of Waterloo Station from 1949 until 1966, when it was transferred to the east end of WESTMINSTER BRIDGE [2E 62d].

Cobden, Richard (1804-65) Leader of the Anti-Corn Law League, Member of Parliament for Stockport, West Riding of Yorkshire and Stockdale, he did much towards the repeal of the Corn Laws in 1846. Because he negotiated a commercial treaty in 1860 with France, Napoleon III defrayed most of the cost of his statue in CAMDEN HIGH STREET [3E 45]. He lived at 23 SUFFOLK STREET, Haymarket [4D 60d].

Cockneys' Church All those born within the sound

St. Mary-le-Bow. The heart of Cockney London.

of Bow Bells (sometimes called 'The Whittington Bells') are Cockneys. ST MARY-LE-BOW, CHEAPSIDE [3E 61b], which houses these famous bells, was built by Sir Christopher Wren in 1670-83. The name Le Bow comes from the original church which was built on arches, or bows, in about 1090; the original Norman crypt still extends under the church. Because of bomb damage in 1941 the church was not opened for worship again until it was restored in 1964.

Cockspur Street, Trafalgar Square [4D 60d] Here one purchased sharp steel spurs to be attached to fighting cocks which fought until one or both were killed. There was a nearby-cockpit in WHITEHALL. Parliament abolished this savage sport in 1849.

Coffee House London's first coffee house was opened in 1657 by Pasqua Rosee in St Michael's Alley, Cornhill [3F 61b]. He called it 'At the Sign of My Own Head'.

Coleman Street, City [2E 61b] In 1642 five members of Cromwell's party, who were accused of treason by Charles I, took refuge here after he had attempted to arrest them in Parliament.

Coleridge, Samuel Taylor (1772-1834) Poet, critic and philosopher, friend of William Wordsworth. His best-known poems are 'The Ancient Mariner', 'Christabel' and 'Kubla Khan', and the best of his criticism is in the *Biographia Literaria.* He lived at 71 BERNERS STREET, Oxford Street [2C 60c] and died at 3 THE GROVE, HIGHGATE VILLAGE [3C 28].

Compton Street, Clerkenwell [4B 46] Named after the Compton family whose residence, the old manor house of Clerkenwell, stood on the site of the former Northampton Polytechnic which in 1966 became the

City University.

Conrad, Joseph (1857-1924) Novelist. Born in the Ukraine of Polish parents. He worked in the British Merchant Navy and became a naturalized British subject in 1884. His most famous novels are *Lord Jim*, *Nostromo*, *Under Western Eyes* and *The Secret Agent*. He lived 1893-6 at 17 GILLINGHAM STREET, Victoria [3B 62c].

Conservatives May Day The first Conservative May Day Rally was held in TRAFALGAR SQUARE on Sunday, 4 May 1969. One of the main speakers was Quintin Hogg (Lord Hailsham), MP for Marylebone and grandson of Quintin Hogg, the founder of Regent Street Polytechnic.

Constable, John (1776-1837) Landscape painter. He became a student at the Royal Academy in 1799. Among his best-known works are 'Flatford Mill', 'Hampstead Heath', 'The Haywain' and 'The Cornfield'. He lived from 1822 until his death at 76 CHARLOTTE STREET, Tottenham Court Road [1C 60c], and is buried in ST JOHN'S CHURCH, CHURCH ROW, HAMPSTEAD [1A 44].

Constable of the Tower Was in command of the TOWER OF LONDON (*see main entry*) garrison and armoury, and responsible for the defence of the Thames round London. He had special powers over the boroughs of Hackney, Shoreditch (now both Hackney), Bethnal Green, Poplar and Stepney (now Tower Hamlets).

Cook, Captain James (1728-79) Seaman and explorer. He charted the coasts of Newfoundland and New Zealand and the east coast of Australia, named New South Wales, Botany Bay, etc. and discovered the Norfolk Islands. He was killed by natives in Hawaii. He lived at 88 MILE END ROAD [1F 61d]. Monument in the MALL erected by Thomas Brock in 1914.

Copyright The first English Copyright Act was established in 1709, but there was some protection of copyright before them. In 1757, when George II helped to enlarge the BRITISH MUSEUM (*see main entry*) by donating his library, the museum also gained the privilege of Compulsory Copyright Deposit, which means that it receives a free copy of every publication in the country.

Coram's Fields and Coram Street, Bloomsbury [1E 60d] Named after Captain Thomas Coram (1688-1751), an English sea captain. Because of his disgust at seeing so many babies being deserted, he established the FOUNDLING HOSPITAL. He donated such large sums of money to charities, including helping the English unemployed in Nova Scotia, that in the end he had to be helped himself. Buried in the chapel of the Foundling Hospital, near his statue in Coram's Fields.

Corn Exchange, Mark Lane, City [4A 61c] Opened in 1747 near its present site, rebuilt in 1880. During building works in 1827 the workmen uncovered a Roman pavement. The establishment was badly damaged by bombs in 1941 and reopened in 1953. It is not only the main market for cereals, but it also deals in animal foods and fertilizers, and imports and exports these raw materials all over the world.

Corps of Commissionaires Founded in 1859 by Captain Edward Walter. Annoyed that so many old soldiers who had fought in the Crimea or in the India Mutiny had to live on a bare pittance, he organized a group of ex-servicemen who were available for work, and set up their headquarters in EXCHANGE COURT, STRAND [4E 60d].

Corsican Hero Pasquale De Paoli (1726-1807), known as the father or hero of Corsica, devoted himself to fighting the Genoese and the French, his country's enemies. He was forced to leave his native land and sought asylum in England. Buried in ST PANCRAS OLD CHURCH, KING'S CROSS [4F 45].

Corsican King In 1736 Theodore I (1696-1756) became King of Corsica. Afraid of being assassinated, he gave up the throne and came to live in Soho. He was sent to King's Bench Prison for debt and died penniless three days after his release. He would have been given a pauper's funeral, but for the generosity of a local tradesman, who had him buried in ST ANNE'S CHURCH, DEAN STREET, Soho [3D 60d].

Costermongers' Church ST MARY MAGDALEN, the parish church of Bermondsey, at the junction of BERMONDSEY STREET and LONG LANE [2A 63c], was built in 1290 on or near the site of Bermondsey Abbey and rebuilt four centuries later. In this church, in September, the costermongers hold their harvest festival, attended by the pearly king and queen.

Covent Garden [3E 60d] The principal market for fruit, vegetables and flowers in London. Covent Garden is a corruption of the 'convent garden' belonging to the Abbots of Westminster. The market originated casually; vendors of fruit and vegetables used the centre of the square for selling their produce and, in time, the market grew into a recognized institution. It is soon to be moved to Nine Elms, near Vauxhall.

Covent Garden Market.

County Hall, Westminster Bridge [1F 62d] Headquarters of the Greater London Council, presumed to be the largest municipal governing body in the world. The building, which was begun in 1909, opened in 1922 for the London County Council and completed in 1933, occupies nine floors, has about 1,500 rooms and covers about six and a half acres. The LCC was created under an Act of Parliament in 1888 and in 1965 was superseded by the Greater London Council which held its first meeting at County Hall on 27 April 1965. The GLC is, in conjunction with the borough councils, responsible for such matters as housing, traffic, fire and ambulance services and parks.

Cranbourn Street, Leicester Square [3E 60d] Formerly called Cranbourn Alley, known to be in existence in 1677 and enlarged to a street in 1844. In this alley William Hogarth (*see main entry*), the artist and engraver, was apprenticed to a goldsmith.

Crane, Walter (1845-1915) Artist. Influenced by the Pre-Raphaelites and most famous as a book illustrator. He was the first president of the Arts Workers Guild, principal of the Royal College of Art and president of the Arts and Crafts Exhibition Society. He lived at 13 HOLLAND STREET, Kensington Church Street [3F 59].

Crazy Gang In 1931 a group of comedians under the leadership of Bud Flanagan joined forces and ran their first Crazy Gang Show at the LONDON PALLADIUM (*see Music Halls*). From 1947 until May 1962, when they disbanded, they performed with some minor interruptions at the VICTORIA PALACE THEATRE, Victoria Street [3B 62c]. (*See also Arches.*)

Cremorne Pleasure Gardens Gave their name to CREMORNE ROAD [2A 76], near the World's End, Chelsea. The name came from Thomas Dawson, Lord Cremorne (*d.* 1813), whose residence, Cremorne House, stood here. The Pleasure Gardens opened in 1843, but owing to rowdyism were forced to close in 1877. In 1904 the Lots Road Power Station, which supplies much of the power for the London Transport Board, was built on the garden site.

Cricket Some form of the game has been played since the thirteenth century and it is known to have been played by Guildford schoolboys in 1550. Possibly the first match to be recorded was played on CLAPHAM COMMON, and an account was published in the *Post Boy* in March, 1700. London's first professional Sunday game, Middlesex *v.* Hampshire, was played on 2 July 1967 at Lord's Cricket Ground. There are regular matches during the cricket season at LORD'S, ST JOHN'S WOOD [4B 44], and the OVAL, KENNINGTON [1A 78].

Cripplegate One of the gates of the City, demolished in 1760, which stood on or near the site of Roman House, WOOD STREET [3D 61b].

Criterion, Piccadilly Circus [4C 60c] Built on the site of an old coaching inn. The restaurant was opened in 1873 by Messrs Spiers and Pond (well-known caterers and managers of the first Australian cricket team to tour Britain). The theatre, built entirely underground, first opened in 1874 and was rebuilt in 1903, it was part of the original Criterion Restaurant and Hotel.

Cromwell, Oliver (1599-1658) Married in 1620 at St Giles' Church, Cripplegate, City. Became an MP in 1628. During the Civil War, he led the Parliamentary troops known as Roundheads and defeated the King's army at Preston in 1649. In 1653 he was appointed Lord Protector by a group of soldiers and civilians. During his Protectorate, Jamaica was added to The British Empire. Died in WHITEHALL PALACE. Monument in the gardens of the HOUSE OF COMMONS.

Crookes, Sir William (1832-1919) Scientist, President of the Royal Society. Wrote a number of books on chemical subjects, and invented the radiometer and Crookes' tube, which is used in X-ray techniques. He discovered the metal thallium. He lived from 1880 until his death at 7 KENSINGTON PARK GARDENS, Notting Hill [2E 59].

Crosby Square, Bishopsgate [3A 61c] Named after Sir John Crosby, who in 1466 built Crosby House there.

The house was burnt down in the seventeenth century, but the hall survived and was moved to CHEYNE WALK, Chelsea, where it was reconstructed in 1910. Sir John, who died in 1475, was a Member of Parliament, Alderman and Sheriff to the City of London. He is buried in ST HELEN'S, BISHOPSGATE (*see City Abbey*).

Crown Jewels These were kept in the Treasury of WESTMINSTER ABBEY until the fourteenth century, when they were stolen by a gang under the leadership of Richard Podicote, who was caught and flayed alive. After that, the jewels were transferred to the TOWER OF LONDON (*see main entry*). On 9 May 1671 Colonel Blood stole the crown, though not the jewels, and was caught on Tower Hill. The king granted the colonel a free pardon and also restored his confiscated estate to him.

Crutched Friars, near Fenchurch Street [3A 61c] The name comes from a now vanished house of Crutched Friars or Friars of the Holy Cross, founded in about 1298.

Cubitt, Thomas (1788-1855) Journeyman and carpenter, who became a master builder and was responsible for the layout of BELGRAVIA, PIMLICO and parts of BLOOMSBURY. He erected a workmen's library and a schoolroom for their children, and was one of the earliest employers to supply his workers with a canteen. He lived at 3 LYALL STREET, off Eaton Square, Belgravia [3F 62b].

Cumberland GREAT CUMBERLAND PLACE, dating from about 1774, and CUMBERLAND GATE, Marble Arch [3E 60b], are both named after the second son of George II, the Duke of Cumberland (1721-65). When he commanded the English army at Culloden in 1764 his needless severity towards the Highlanders earned him the title of 'Butcher'.

Curzon, George, Marquess (1859-1925) Viceroy of India 1899-1905, Secretary of State for Foreign Affairs 1918-22, author and archaeologist with a special interest in the ancient monuments of India. He lived from 1894 until his death at 1 CARLTON HOUSE TERRACE, Pall Mall [1C 62c]. There is a statue at the corner of Carlton Gardens.

Cutty Sark The last and greatest of all sailing clippers was launched in Dumbarton on the Clyde in November 1869. This ship was used as a wool carrier to Australia and to bring crops of tea from China. She was sold to the Portuguese in 1895, and returned to Greenwich Pier in 1954, where she is permanently berthed [1D 81]. She is now used as a museum and as an educational centre for the Merchant Navy.

The Cutty Sark.

D

Dance, George George Dance the Elder (1700-68), architect, designed Mansion House. George Dance the Younger (1741-1825), his son, also an architect, was one of the founder members of the Royal Academy; he rebuilt Newgate Prison in 1770, held the office of City Architect and Surveyor of Works and built the façade of the Guildhall, City. He lived and died at 91 Gower Street, Bloomsbury [1D 60d]. Buried in St Paul's Cathedral.

Darby and Joan This phrase for a devoted old couple was probably first used in 1735 in a song; a Mr Woodfall wrote a ballad about his employer, John Darby, and his wife, who were always dressed in black and lived in Bartholomew Close, near Bart's Hospital, City.

Darwin, Charles (1809-82) Scientist whose name is always linked with the theory of evolution. He travelled as a naturalist with HMS *Beagle* in the southern hemisphere and wrote *The Origin of Species* and *The Descent of Man*. He lived 1839-42 at 110 Gower Street, Bloomsbury [1D 60d], now the new extension of University College. Buried in Westminster Abbey.

Das Kapital Karl Heinrich Marx (1818-83), German philosopher and social economist, was expelled from Germany and France for political reasons. He came to London in 1849 and lived at 4 Anderson Street,

Chelsea [4D 62b]. He was evicted a year later for rent arrears and from 1850-6 lived at 28 DEAN STREET, Soho [2D 60d], where he wrote *Das Kapital*. Buried in HIGHGATE CEMETERY.

Defoe, Daniel (1660-1731) Novelist and journalist. Born in FORE STREET, City [2E 61b], and married in 1683 at ST BOTOLPH'S, ALDERSGATE [2D 61b]. He joined William of Orange to soldier in 1688. His pamphlet *The Shortest Way to Dissenters* earned him a spell in Newgate Prison. Author of *Robinson Crusoe*, *Journal of the Plague Year* and *Moll Flanders*. He lived at DEFOE ROAD, Stoke Newington [4D 31] and died in ROPEMAKER STREET, Moorgate [1E 61b]. Buried in BUNHILL FIELDS, Moorgate.

Democratic Earl Simon De Montfort (*d.* 1265), Earl of Leicester, sometimes known as the founder of democracy, lived in the PALACE OF SAVOY (*see main entry*); there is a memorial tablet attached to the Savoy Hotel which stands on the site of the palace. In 1264, on his orders, writs were issued to barons, sheriffs, burgesses and citizens to attend the first parliament, and the first assembly met in January 1265. The earl was killed at the Battle at Evesham.

De Morgan, William (1839-1917) Novelist and pre-Raphaelite artist. Born in London and educated at University College. His work in pottery and glass was much admired. When he retired he took up writing, producing *Joseph Vance* at the age of sixty-six, followed closely by further novels. He lived at 125 OLD CHURCH STREET, Chelsea [1B 76].

Denmark Hill, Camberwell. With nearby DOG KENNEL HILL [3C 78] this was a favourite hunting ground for Prince George of Denmark (1653-1708), husband of Queen Anne and second son of Frederick III of

Denmark. The Prince, of whom it is said that he was neither liked or disliked by the English public, is buried in WESTMINSTER ABBEY.

Deptford Incorporated in the Borough of Lewisham. Derives its name from '*depeford*', the deep ford over the River Ravensbourne (*see Ravensbourne*). This borough, the home of the lovely flower, the Deptford Pink, was noted for its naval dockyard, founded by Henry VII (1457-1509) in 1485 and closed in 1869.

Detective Novel's Debut William Wilkie Collins (1824-89) in 1860 wrote *The Woman in White* and is acclaimed as the first British novelist to deal with the detection of crime. His most famous later novel is *The Moonstone*. He lived 1863-76 and 1883-6 at 65 GLOUCESTER PLACE, Marylebone [1E 60b], and died at 82 WIMPOLE STREET [2A 60c]. Buried in KENSAL GREEN CEMETERY.

Devonshire Club Founded in 1874 at 50 ST JAMES'S STREET, Piccadilly [4B 60c], formerly the home of Crockford's Club, as a Liberal club by the Marquess of Hartingdon, later Duke of Devonshire. The Marquess named the club after his father, who was its first president, and up to the present day all successive holders of the title have been presidents of the club.

Dickens, Charles (1812-1870) Novelist. As a schoolboy, he lived in BAYHAM STREET, Camden Town [1D 63], and while still very young he had to work for a time in a blacking factory in south London. He became a lawyer's clerk and then worked as a reporter for the *Morning Chronicle*. His most famous novels are probably *David Copperfield*, *Oliver Twist*, *Bleak House* and *The Old Curiosity Shop*. In 1836 he was married in ST LUKE'S, CHELSEA. He lived 1837-9 at 48 DOUGHTY STREET, Bloomsbury [4F 45], now a

National Trust House, 1838-51 at the junction [3C 62] of MARYLEBONE HIGH STREET and Marylebone Road (house now demolished) and 1851-60 in TAVISTOCK SQUARE, Euston [4E 45] (site now occupied by the British Medical Association). Buried in WESTMINSTER ABBEY.

Dictionary Dr Samuel Johnson (1709-84) came to London in 1737 and worked for the *Gentleman's Magazine*. In 1747 he started work on his *Dictionary*, published in 1755. His other works include *Lives of the Poets*. He lived 1748-59 at 17 GOUGH SQUARE, off Fleet Street [3B 61a], now a museum. He died in BOLT COURT, Fleet Street and is buried in WESTMINSTER ABBEY. Statue outside ST CLEMENT DANES, STRAND [3A 61a].

Lord Beaconsfield

Dr. Samuel Johnson.

Dilke, Sir Charles (1843-1911) Member of Parliament for Chelsea 1868-86. In 1885 his political career was ended by his unfortunate appearance as co-respondent in a divorce case. Author of *Greater Britain*, advocating the union of the United States and the British Empire. He was born, lived and died at 76 SLOANE STREET [2E 62b].

Diplomatic Wives On 31 May 1962, for the first time, wives of the London ambassadors accompanied their husbands to a dinner held by the foreign secretary at LANCASTER HOUSE to celebrate the Queen's official birthday.

Dirty Dick's The tavern at 202 BISHOPSGATE [2A 61c] A Nathaniel Bentley lived and owned a hardware store in Leadenhall Street; on the eve of their wedding day his fiancée died and so Bentley, who had been something of a dandy, closed the room where the wedding breakfast lay and became a recluse. Forty years later, when he died, the contents were moved to the tavern now known as Dirty Dick's.

Disraeli, Benjamin (1804-81) Conservative statesman and novelist. Born at 22 THEOBALD'S ROAD, Bloomsbury [1F 60d], of Italian-Jewish parentage, but baptized a Christian at the age of twelve at ST ANDREW'S, HOLBORN VIADUCT [2B 61a]. In 1837 he was elected Conservative MP for Maidstone. He first became prime minister in 1868, and was so again 1874-80. He was responsible for the proclamation of Queen Victoria as Empress of India and for the government's purchase of the controlling shares in the Suez Canal. His novels include *Sybil* and *Coningsby*. He lived 1839-73 at 93 PARK LANE [3E 60b] and died at 19 CURZON STREET, Mayfair [4A 60c]. Statue in PARLIAMENT SQUARE.

Dogget Coat and Badge Race Thomas Dogget (*d.* 1721), actor, singer and manager of Drury Lane

Theatre, in 1716 founded the Dogget Coat and Badge Race. Six watermen just out of their apprenticeship take part and the race must be rowed against the tide. The course, from London Bridge to Cadogan Pier, Chelsea, is just under four and a half miles.

Dog Racing London's first greyhound race meeting was held on 20 June 1927 at the WHITE CITY, Shepherd's Bush [2C 58]. The Harringay track opened on 13 September in the same year. The Greyhound 'Derby' takes place at White City in June.

Dogs' Cemetery In 1880 the Duke of Cambridge buried his wife's dog in HYDE PARK, near Victoria Gate, Bayswater Road. From then until the little cemetery closed in 1915 there were some three hundred canine burials.

Domesday Book A survey of England made by William the Conqueror in 1086. It included records of ownership and assessments of land, tenants and livestock, etc. The manuscripts can be seen in the museum of the PUBLIC RECORDS OFFICE, Chancery Lane (*see Chancery Lane*).

Double-Decker Train British Rail's first and last double-decker train, which was designed to increase passenger seating by 30 per cent went into operation between London and Dartford in 1949. It made its last journey on 1 October 1971, when it pulled out of Charing Cross Station to take commuters to Dartford on the Bexleyheath line before being scrapped.

Downing Street [1E 62d] Named after Sir George Downing (1623-84) who was for a time Secretary to the Treasury with Pepys, the diarist (*see main entry*), as his clerk. In 1681, he bought some ground in Whitehall and built four houses. Sir Robert Walpole, the country's first prime minister in the modern sense, used No. 10 as his official residence in 1735 and it has been the home of all prime ministers since then.

Dryden Street, Drury Lane [3E 60d] Named in honour of John Dryden (1631-1700), poet, dramatist and satirist. Educated at Westminster School. In 1668, he was appointed Poet Laureate but he lost the position in 1688. His best-known works are 'Absalom and Achitophel', 'Annus Mirabilis' and 'The Hind and the Panther'. He died at 43 GERRARD STREET, Shaftesbury Avenue [3D 60d], and is buried in WESTMINSTER ABBEY.

Dulwich College, Dulwich Common [2C 94] Originally founded by Edward Alleyn (1566-1626), actor and proprietor of several playhouses. Baptized in ST BOTOLPH'S, BISHOPSGATE [2A 61c], in the parish where he was born. He purchased the manor of Dulwich and founded the College of God's Gift, a trust which now maintains Dulwich College and Dulwich College Picture Gallery. He is buried in the chapel of the college. ALLEYN PARK and ALLEYN ROAD near the College honour his name.

Dutch Church, Austinfriars, Old Broad Street [2F 61b] Built on the site of an Augustian Friary. In 1550, King Edward VI (1547-53) granted permission to the fugitives from Holland living in London to use this church as their place of worship. The church was destroyed in the blitz of 1940 and rebuilt in 1954. Since then services on Sunday have been held in Dutch.

E

Ealing Abbey, Charlbury Grove, Ealing [1A 56] Opened on 12 July 1962, this was the first Benedictine abbey to be built in London since 1539. The abbey is a restoration and enlargement of the church of St Benedict, built early this century and partially destroyed by bombs in the Second World War.

Eaton Square, Belgravia [3F 62b] Built in about 1827 by Thomas Cubitt (*see main entry*) in the area known as the Five Fields. It is named after Eaton Hall, in Cheshire, the principal seat of Lord Grosvenor, Duke of Westminster. This pleasant square, over a quarter of a mile in length, was the residence of Stanley Baldwin (No. 93) and Neville Chamberlain (No. 37), two British prime ministers; George Peabody, the American philanthropist died at No. 80.

Edward VII (1841-1910) Born and died in BUCKINGHAM PALACE. Eldest son of Queen Victoria, he married Princess Alexandra, eldest daughter of the King of Denmark and came to the throne in 1901. For his diplomacy, he earned the name 'Edward the Peacemaker'. A great sportsman, winner of the Derby three times. During his duties, he travelled to India, Russia, Italy and France. Monument in WATERLOO PLACE, Lower Regent Street [4D 60d].

Electric Exhibition, The The first exhibition of electrical lighting apparatus ever held was inaugurated at the ROYAL ALBERT HALL by King Edward VII, then Prince of Wales, on 7 May 1879.

Eaton Square, Belgravia.

Electrician Extraordinary (especially Electrical Transformers) Michael Faraday (1791-1867) was first apprenticed as a bookbinder from 1805-12 at 48 BLANDFORD STREET, Baker Street [2E 60b], but in 1813 he became Sir Humphry Davy's assistant at the Royal Institution and in 1827 he succeeded him as professor of chemistry there. He is noted for his epoch-making discoveries in all fields of electricity. Faraday was the first secretary of the Athenaeum Club, PALL MALL, a post he held for a year. Buried in HIGHGATE CEMETERY [4D 29].

Elephant and Castle [3C 63a] The name is a corruption of The Infanta of Castile, a tavern named after a Spanish princess who fled to England to escape the Spanish Inquisition and stayed at an inn near the Elephant. Some hold that the name is derived from the sign, showing an Elephant with a castle on its back, which was used by the CUTLER'S Co, who used to trade here.

Elgar, Sir Edward (1857-1934) Composer. Largely a self-taught musician, he came to London in 1889. His most famous works are the *Enigma Variations*, *The*

Dream of Gerontius and the *Pomp and Circumstances* marches. He was knighted in 1904. He lived 1890-1 at 51 AVONMORE ROAD, West Kensington [4E 59].

Eliot, George (1819-80) The pen name of Mary Anne Evans, novelist. From 1851-3 she was assistant editor of the *Westminster Review*. She won fame with her novels, such as *Adam Bede*, *The Mill on the Floss*, *Silas Marner* and her masterpiece *Middlemarch*. She lived the last few weeks of her life and died at 4 CHEYNE WALK, Chelsea [1A 76]. Buried in HIGHGATE CEMETERY.

Elizabeth 1 (1533-1603) Born at GREENWICH (*see main entry*), daughter of Henry VIII and Anne Boleyn, she succeeded to the throne in 1558. Plots to kill her and replace her with Mary, Queen of Scots were discovered and Mary was executed. The defeat of the Spanish Armada during her reign made England supreme on the sea. A statue of her was originally erected on the Lud Gate in 1586 and moved to ST DUNSTAN-IN-THE-WEST, Fleet Street [3B 61a], in 1766. Her statue is thought to be the oldest in this country. She died at the Richmond Palace (since demolished) and is buried in WESTMINSTER ABBEY.

Ely Place, Holborn [2B 61a] Laid out in 1775 on part of the site of a palace of the Bishops of Ely (demolished in 1773). ST ETHELDREDA'S in Ely Place was the private chapel of the bishops and was the first pre-Reformation church in London to revert back to the Roman Catholic Church.

Enclosed Market MARK LANE, Eastcheap [4A 61c], is a corruption of Market Lane. Until 1751, the corn merchants did their business in coffee houses and taverns near Aldgate. Then they got together and built the enclosed market on the site of the present

Corn Exchange in Mark Lane. In 1872 the Exchange received the Royal Charter from Queen Victoria.

Eros, Piccadilly Circus [4C 60c] The Shaftesbury memorial or The Angel of Christian Charity. It was designed by Sir Alfred Gilbert and erected in 1893 as a memorial to the seventh Earl of Shaftesbury (1801-85), who introduced measures in Parliament protecting children working as chimney sweeps and in mills, and preventing women and children working down the mines.

Escalators Earls Court Station had the first tube escalator in the world on its premises, built in 1911. Leicester Square escalator, 161ft 6ins long, with a

Eros. A memorial to the man concerned about child labour.

vertical rise of 80ft 9ins, is the longest of any tube. Chancery Lane has one 30ft long with a vertical risk of 15ft, which is the shortest.

Evelyn Street, Deptford [4A 64] Commemorates the name of John Evelyn (1620-1706), famed for his diary which covers his whole life and such events as the Plague and the Great Fire. He was Treasurer of Greenwich Hospital and lived 1695-1703 at the manor of Sayes Court, Deptford, the house he loaned to Peter the Great (*see main entry*) in 1698 (its site is indicated by SAYES PARK).

Execution Block In the garden of TRINITY SQUARE, Tower Hill [4A 61c], stood the old scaffold, where between 1388 and 1747 many were executed for high treason. During the last execution, that of Lord Lovat, the last man to be beheaded in England, the scaffolding that had been erected for the spectators collapsed, killing twelve people.

F

Female Judge On 8 October 1962, at the High Court, Strand, Her Honour Judge Elizabeth Lane QC became the first woman ever to sit as a Divorce Commissioner. Helping her were a court associate and shorthand writer, both women. By coincidence, the first three cases were by women petitioners.

Film Industry Wardour Street, Soho [3C 60c] is the centre of the film industry in London and contains the headquarters of the great motion picture companies. It is named after Lord Arundel of Wardour, the ground landlord, who married the daughter of Colonel Panton the gambler (*see Panton Street*).

Film Pioneer William Friese-Green (1855-1921), pioneer of cinematography, made what may have been the first motion picture ever at Hyde Park Corner in 1888. He was ruined by his experiments and had to serve a prison sentence for debt. He lived at 138 Maida Vale [3F 43]. Buried in Highgate Cemetery.

First Church The church of St Peter, on the corner of Cornhill and Gracechurch Street [3F 61b], stands on the site of the oldest church in London. It is said to have been founded by King Lucius in about AD 179. It was re-built by Sir Christopher Wren in 1677-87.

Fish and Chips The first known fish and chip shop was opened by Joseph Malin in 1860 in Cleveland Way, Mile End Road. In 1875 the family moved to

560 OLD FORD ROAD, Bow, where they ran the business until 8 July 1972, when it was closed by the Tower Hamlets Council under a compulsory purchase order.

Fish Festival Every October, the Billingsgate Traders celebrate their Fish Harvest Festival at ST MARY-AT-HILL, EASTCHEAP [4F 61b]. This church, which gave the street that it is in its name was built 1670-6 by Sir Christopher Wren, to replace the one partly destroyed in the fire of 1666.

Fishmongers' Hall The Fishmongers' Company, one of the oldest of the twelve great livery companies, has the right to weigh and examine fish for sale and to prosecute if necessary. The Fishmongers' Hall in KING WILLIAM STREET, London Bridge [3F 61b], was the first livery hall to burn in the fire of 1666 and the first to be set on fire again by enemy bombs in September 1940.

Flask Walk, Hampstead [1A 44] Derives its name from a house later converted to a tavern that sold flasks of spring water, famed for its medicinal qualities.

Fleet Street [3B 61a] The home of the national newspapers and many of the larger provincial ones. It takes its name from the old Fleet River that ran from Hampstead Heath via Holborn into the Thames at Blackfriars Bridge. In 1765 the City Corporation covered over the river.

Floating Hall The *Wellington*, a former New Zealand Navy sloop moored off Victoria Embankment [4A 61a], now serves as the livery hall of the Master Mariners. This worshipful company, the only one to have a floating hall, is the most junior of the city livery companies.

Floating Museum On 21 October 1971 Mr P. Kirk, Minister for the Royal Navy, handed over the *Belfast*, the 11,550-ton cruiser, to the HMS *Belfast* Trust. During the ceremony, some officers from the German battle cruiser *Scharnhorst* which fought the *Belfast* in 1943 stood side by side with the British admirals. The *Belfast*, the largest cruiser ever built for the Royal Navy, will be administered as a floating museum, the first of its kind. It is now permanently moored on the Thames, near TOWER BRIDGE [4B 61c]. Entrance in Vine Lane.

Flyover HOLBORN VIADUCT [2C 61a], constructed almost entirely of iron, was built by the City Corporation and opened by Queen Victoria on 6 November 1869, the same day as Blackfriars Bridge. The four bronze statues on top of the pedestals represent Agriculture, Commerce, Science and Fine Arts. The viaduct, 1,400 ft long and 80 ft wide, may be considered a forerunner of modern flyovers.

Foch, Marshal Ferdinand (1851-1929) Enlisted in the French army during the Franco-Prussian War and corps commander in Lorraine in 1914. In 1918 he was appointed commander in chief of the Allied armies, and in July he launched the Allied offensive which ended the war. Statue in GROSVENOR GARDENS opposite Victoria Station [3A 62c].

Football Cup Final The first football Cup Final was played in the 1871-2 season at the OVAL, Kennington [1A 78], the home of the Surrey Cricket Club. The game, between the Wanderers and the Royal Engineers, ended with the former winning 1-0. The first all-London football Cup Final, Chelsea *v.* Tottenham Hotspurs, was fought out on 20 May 1967 at WEMBLEY STADIUM (*see main entry*), with the latter winning 2-1.

The Football Association Cup Final takes place at Wembley Stadium in late April or early May.

Footstool Church ST JOHN'S, SMITH SQUARE, Millbank [3E 62d], was built by Thomas Archer 1713-28. Many people claim that Queen Anne kicked a footstool upside down and this gave the architect his inspiration for its design, hence its nickname, the Footstool Church. It was bombed during the Second World War but has been restored and is now used as an arts centre. (*See also Smith Square*.)

Fortnum and Mason, Piccadilly [4C 60c] High-class grocer. It was founded in 1707 by William Fortnum, Member of Parliament and footman to Queen Anne, and his cousin, Hugh Mason. Fortnum looked after the groceries and Mason the stables (hence MASON'S YARD near the stores in Duke Street). In November 1964 the store acquired the large clock that stands above the main entrance with its two 4ft effigies representing the original owners.

Fox, Charles James (1749-1806) Member of Parliament 1769-1806, elected leader of the Whig Party in 1775. He was a great orator famed for his debating powers. He lived at 46 CLARGES STREET, Piccadilly [4A 60c]. There is a statue of him in BLOOMSBURY SQUARE [2E 60d] with the Magna Carta in his hand. He died at CHISWICK HOUSE (*see main entry*).

Franklin, Benjamin (1706-90) Statesman and scientist. Born in Boston, USA. He helped to draw up the American Declaration of Independence and to draft the US constitution. He discovered that lightning was a form of electricity and invented the lightning conductor. He came to London in 1724 and lived in LITTLE BRITAIN, City [2D 61b], and later at 36 CRAVEN STREET, Strand [4E 60d].

Free Education LANCASTER STREET, off the Borough Road [2C 63a], is named after Joseph Lancaster, who was born in 1778 in the borough of Southwark. In 1796, his father provided him with a room in which he taught ninety poor children free. He educated the older and more intelligent pupils, who, in turn, taught the younger and less able. Dejected that promises made to him to aid free education were broken, he left in 1820 for America, where friends and industry helped him in his project in the States.

Free French When General de Gaulle escaped from France in the Second World War, he came to London and established the Free French Army. On 1 July 1940 he opened their headquarters at 4 CARLTON GARDENS, Pall Mall [1C 62c]. Members of the Free French resistance movement were trained at their headquarters at 1 DORSET SQUARE, Marylebone [1E 60b]. The Free French naval headquarters were from 1940-5 at STAFFORD HOUSE, STAFFORD PLACE, Victoria [2B 62c].

Free Snuff Near the entrance to the Chamber of the HOUSE OF COMMONS is a snuff box used by members to keep awake during late sittings. The tradition of free snuff started in the middle of the nineteenth century when an MP left a bequest for it. The legacy has since run out and the Exchequer footed the bill until early in 1970 when a Liverpool tobacco firm agreed to supply the snuff free.

French Poet Stéphane Mallarmé (1842-98), the French poet whose works include *L'Apres-Midi d'un Faune*, which inspired the composer Debussy, lived in 1863 at 6 BROMPTON SQUARE, Knightsbridge [2C 62a].

Fry, Elizabeth (1780-1845) Prison reformer, daughter of a Quaker banker. She organized night shelters for the homeless. In 1813 she visited NEWGATE PRISON, and, horrified by what she saw, set out to reform the conditions. In 1818 she was thanked for her good work by a committee in the House of Commons. She lived from 1800-9 at ST MILDRED'S COURT, Poultry [3E 61b].

Fulham Palace, Fulham Palace Road [1C 74] The residence of the Bishops of London, who owned the Manor of Fulham from about 690 until 1868. The entrance courtyard was built by Bishop FitzJames in the reign of Henry VII and the rest of the buildings were erected in the eighteenth and nineteenth centuries. CHANCELLORS ROAD, off the Fulham Palace Road, was originally a copse or wood that Ralph de Ivinghoe gave as a gift to the Chancellor of St Paul's Cathedral.

Fulham Pottery Thought to be the oldest in the world, founded by John Dwight at 210 NEW KING'S ROAD [3E 75]. In April 1671, he took out a patent for the earthenware figures, statues etc., which were never made anywhere else in the world.

G

Galleons There is a model of a galleon on every lamp in the MALL [1C 62c]. They were erected by Thomas Brock in 1913 to go with the Queen Victoria Memorial (*see Wedding Cake*), but he left no explanation as to why he chose this ship.

Gallery Inn Before James Burbage built the first theatres, plays were staged in the gallery inns. The

The George. Last of the gallery inn theatres.

George, the last of the gallery inns, at 77 BOROUGH HIGH STREET [2D 63b], was originally called the St George and the Dragon. It is known to have been in existence in 1554, owned by a Mr Colet, a Member of Parliament. Gutted by fire in 1676 and rebuilt the following year, it is now controlled by the National Trust Fund.

Garrick, David (1717-79) Actor. Particularly famous for his performances as Richard III and Hamlet. He was part-manager of the Drury Lane Theatre, where he produced a number of Shakespeare's plays and he wrote some lively farces himself. In 1749 he married a dancer at ST GILES-IN-THE-FIELDS, ST GILES'S CIRCUS [2D 60d]. He lived 1750-72 at 27 SOUTHAMPTON STREET, Strand [3F 60d]. Buried in WESTMINSTER ABBEY.

Geffrye Museum, Kingsland Road, Shoreditch [4D 47] It occupies the Ironmongers' Almshouses, which were built in 1715 under a bequest of Sir Robert Geffrye, clerk of the Ironmongers' Company and Lord Mayor of London in 1685, for widows of members of the Company. In 1913 the London County Council took over the property and converted it into a furniture museum. Statue of Sir Robert (*d.*1704) can be seen above the entrance.

George I (1660-1727) Came to the throne on the death of Queen Anne and reigned 1714-27. German-born, he spoke no English and he left the country's administration to his ministers. His reign saw the South Sea Bubble, the financial swindle that caused the ruin of many families. There is a statue of him in a toga on the steeple of ST GEORGE'S CHURCH, BLOOMSBURY WAY [2E 60d].

George II (1683-1760) Son of George I. He reigned 1727-60. In 1743, he fought in the Battle of Dettingen and was the last British monarch to command a battle. He died in KENSINGTON PALACE (*see London Museum*) and is buried in WESTMINSTER ABBEY. Statue in GOLDEN SQUARE (*see main entry*), Soho.

George III (1738-1820) Born in the original NORFOLK HOUSE (*see main entry*), St James's Square. Grandson of George II. His reign which lasted from 1760-1820 was characterized by bribery. Known as 'Farmer George', he became permanently insane in 1811, and his eldest son was appointed Prince Regent. Statue in PALL MALL EAST [4D 60d].

George IV (1762-1830) Eldest son of George III. Born in ST JAMES'S PALACE (*see main entry*). He was noted for his extravagance and debauchery as Prince of Wales. When he was appointed Prince Regent, he went to live at CARLTON HOUSE (*see main entry*). His equestrian statue in TRAFALGAR SQUARE is without saddle and stirrups.

George V (1865-1936) Second son of Edward VII, he became heir to the throne on the death of his elder brother in 1892 and reigned 1910-36. In 1911, he visited India, the first reigning sovereign to do so. His reign was marked by the First World War, the General Strike, and the first Labour government. Statue in OLD PALACE YARD, opposite the House of Lords. To commemorate his Jubilee in 1935, the bend in the Thames between Westminster Bridge and London Bridge was named the KING'S REACH.

George VI (1895-1952) He came to the throne in 1936 when his brother, Edward VIII, abdicated. His reign saw the Second World War and the achievements of Winston Churchill as prime minister. As Duke of York, he lived at 17 BRUTON STREET, Bond Street [4B 60c], and in this house Queen Elizabeth II was born. Before he came to the throne he lived at 145 PICCADILLY. Monument in CARLTON HOUSE TERRACE, Pall Mall [1D 62d].

German poet Heinrich Heine (1797-1856), a poet with revolutionary sympathies, was disappointed with Germany's political regime and migrated to Paris in 1831. His best-known works are the *Reisebilder*, the *Buch Der Leider* and *Atta Troll*. He came to London in 1827 and lived at 32 CRAVEN STREET, Strand [4E 60d].

Gibbon, Edward (1737-94) Historian, born in Putney. Author of *The History of the Decline and Fall of the Roman Empire*. He lived 1773-83 at 7 BENTINCK STREET, Welbeck Street [2A 60c].

Gilbert, Sir William Schwenck (1836-1911) Dramatist. His partnership with Sir Arthur Sullivan (*see main entry*) lasted from 1871 until 1896. They produced a series of comic operas including *HMS Pinafore*, *The Mikado* and *The Gondoliers*, but their collaboration ended because of personal differences. Gilbert lived at 39 HARRINGTON GARDENS, Gloucester Road [4F 59]. His monument, a bronze medallion by Sir G. Frampton, is on the VICTORIA EMBANKMENT [3B 61a].

Giltspur Street, City [2C 61a] The home of BART'S HOSPITAL (*see Hospital*), formerly known as Knightrider Street. Legend has it that it takes its name from the knights who wore gilt spurs and passed by on their way to the tournaments held at Smithfield.

Gin Is a word thought to have been adapted from the French 'Genievre', or Dutch 'Genever'. In 1769 Alexander Gordon, who was already established in business in Clerkenwell, formed a company called 'The House of Gordon' in Goswell Street (now GOSWELL ROAD), Clerkenwell [4B 46]. The building was bombed in May 1941 and rebuilt in 1954. Gordon's maintain that they have the largest gin distillery in the world.

Gladstone, William Ewart (1809-98) Statesman. Entered Parliament in 1838 as a Tory MP but in 1859 became a Liberal and was four times prime minister. Introduced voting by ballot and reforms in education and was a firm believer in Irish Home Rule. He lived at 73 HARLEY STREET [1A 60c] and 11 CARLTON HOUSE TERRACE, Pall Mall [1D 62d], and, in 1890, at CHATHAM HOUSE (*see main entry*), St James's Square. Monument outside ST CLEMENT DANES, STRAND [3A 61a].

'Glasshouse, The' The Daily Express office in FLEET STREET, erected in 1932, was one of the first buildings to have an outsize glass façade. Some journalists call it 'The Glasshouse'.

Gog and Magog The two figures in the GUILDHALL (*see main entry*) are thought to represent the legendary struggle between the ancient Britons and the Trojans. The two previous eighteenth-century effigies, themselves copied of medieval ones, were destroyed by enemy action in December 1940; the modern versions were replaced in the Guildhall by the generosity of Sir George Wilkinson, who was Lord Mayor of London 1940-1.

Golden Square, Soho [3C 60c] Laid out in about 1688 and presumed to have derived its name from a nearby tavern, The Gelding, which in due course changed its name to The Golden.

Goldsmith, Oliver (1728-1774) Irish-born author. His works include the novel *The Vicar of Wakefield*, the play *She Stoops to Conquer* and such poems as 'The Deserted Village'. He lived at 2 BRICK COURT, Temple

(3B 61a), and was buried in the nearby TEMPLE CHURCH, INNER TEMPLE LANE.

Goldsmith's Row, Hackney Road [4E 47] Originally called Mutton Lane, after a nearby tavern, The Cat and the Mutton. In 1703, a Mr Morrel built alms-houses for poor members of the Goldsmiths' Company in this street and the name changed accordingly.

Golf Known to have been played in Scotland in the fifteenth century. Credit is given to James I (1566-1625) for introducing it to England; he first played it here on BLACKHEATH. Founded in 1608, The Royal Blackheath, now at Court Road, ELTHAM, is the oldest golf club in the world.

Gordon, General Charles George (1835-1885) Born in Woolwich, baptized in ST ALPHEGE'S, GREENWICH CHURCH STREET (*see Greenwich*). In 1852, he joined the Royal Engineers and fought in more than thirty battles in the Crimea, China etc. In 1884 he was sent to the Sudan and was besieged and killed at Khartoum. Statue on VICTORIA EMBANKMENT [3B 61a].

Gordon Square, Bloomsbury [1D 60d] Laid out by Thomas Cubitt (*see main entry*) in 1820. The Gothic church of Christ the King in the square was built in 1835 by Raphael Brandon. It is the principal Anglican Church serving London University.

Gospel Oak, Kentish Town [1D 45] So called because in days of old it was the custom to read the gospel aloud under an oak tree which grew on the parish boundary line.

Gracechurch Street, City [3F 61b] Derives its name from the now vanished church of St Benet Grace-church, so called because it was built on a grass or herb market. During the reign of Edward III (r.

1327-77) it was the custom for all carts bringing their produce to the herb market to pay a toll, with the exception of the Hospital of the Priory of St John's and Jerusalem.

Grahame, Kenneth (1859-1932) Author of *The Golden Age*, *Dream Days* and, most famous, the animal fantasy *The Wind in the Willows*. He lived 1901-8 at 16 PHILLIMORE PLACE, Kensington [3E 59].

Grasshopper Vane The weather-vane shaped like a grasshopper on top of the ROYAL EXCHANGE opposite the BANK OF ENGLAND, is the family crest of Sir Thomas Gresham (*see main entry*), the founder of the original building. There is a story, which may, however, be apocryphal, that when he was a small child Sir Thomas got lost and was found by his parents through the chirping of a grasshopper.

Gray, Thomas (1716-71) Poet. Born at 39 CORNHILL, City [3F 61b]. His most famous poem is undoubtedly his 'Elegy written in a Country Churchyard' which refers to Stoke Poges, Bucks, where he is buried.

Great George Street, Parliament Square [2D 62d] Built on the site of a stableyard that belonged to a tavern, The George and Dragon. It was in a house in this street that the body of Lord Byron (*see main entry*) lay in state before being taken for burial.

Great Scotland Yard [4E 60d] Stands on the site of the part of the old Whitehall Palace which housed visiting Scottish royalty. This establishment was the official residence of the royal architects who included Inigo Jones and Vanburgh. From 1842-90 the Metropolitan Police had their headquarters here, but in 1890 they moved to New Scotland Yard, Victoria Embankment. In 1967 they moved to a new block in the Broadway off VICTORIA STREET.

'Great Stink, The' In the warm summer of 1858 the wind from the Thames gave out a horrible stench caused by the sewer gases. During this period most of the river steamers were taken out of service, and on a number of occasions Parliament had to adjourn for the day. Because of the stench it was known as the year of the 'Great Stink'.

Great Titchfield Street, off Oxford Street [1B 60c] is named after William Bentick, Duke of Portland, Marquis of Tichfield. BOLSOVER STREET, near the north side of Gt. Portland Street, is named after the Duke's estate in Derbyshire. Riding House Street, also off Gt. Portland Street, is thought to have been built on a riding academy.

Greedy Boy There are several stories about the statue of the Fat Boy which stands at PYE CORNER [2C 61a], the corner of Cock Lane and Giltspur Street, opposite Bart's Hospital. Some claim it was put to mark the northernmost point reached by the Great Fire of 1666. Others claim that it represents the greedy boy who stole a bun from a baker's shop and accidentally started the fire. Yet another view is that it represents Londoners who were gluttons.

Greek Street, Soho [3D 60d] Built about 1681, it probably derived its name from a colony of Greeks who lived there. The street is now noted for its foreign restaurants.

Greenaway, Kate (1846-1901) Artist and book illustrator, particularly of children's books. Her best-known works are *Under the Willow* and *Mother Goose*. She lived at 39 Frognal, Hampstead [1A 44].

Green Tape In 1926 the GPO requested permission to erect a telephone booth on land belonging to the

Institution of Electrical Engineers. The latter agreed, on condition that the booth was painted green to harmonize with their railings. For two years the Post Office fought for standard red, but lost. So in February 1928 London's only green phone booth was placed at the junction of SAVOY STREET and VICTORIA EMBANKMENT [4F 60d], where it still stands.

Greenwich The birthplace of Henry VIII and his daughters Elizabeth and Mary, is a corruption of Grenevic, the green town. It is presumed that the site of St. Alpheges Church, (Church Street), is where Alphege, Archbishop of Canterbury was martyred by the Danes in 1011.

Gresham, Sir Thomas (1519-79) Merchant and financier, founder of Gresham College in the City. In 1566, he built the first Royal Exchange, which was gutted by the fire of 1666. His name is given to Gresham's Law: bad money drives out good money. He lived at 23 OLD BROAD STREET, Bank [2F 61b]. Buried in ST HELEN'S CHURCH, BISHOPSGATE (*see City Abbey*).

A view of Greenwich, home of the National Maritime Museum.

Greville, Fulke, Lord Brooke (1554-1628) Poet. Servant to Elizabeth I, Chancellor of the Exchequer and Lord of the King's Bedchamber during the reign of James I. Author of *Mustapha* and *Remains*. He was murdered by his servant who then committed suicide. BROOKE STREET and GREVILLE STREET, Holborn [2B 61a], are built on the site of Brooke House, his residence.

Greycoat School, Greycoat Place, Victoria [3C 62c] Founded in 1698 as the Greycoat Hospital by the citizens of Westminster for the education of 110 poor boys and girls. The school was so named because of the clothing worn by the inmates. In 1873 it became a school for girls only. In the Second World War it was damaged by bombs, but it has since been restored.

Grosvenor Square, Mayfair [3F 60b] Built originally 1720-30, but extensively rebuilt in recent years. It takes its name from Sir Richard Grosvenor (*d.* 1732). On the west side of the square stands the American Embassy, built in 1960. (*See also Little America.*)

Grote, George (1794-1871) Historian and banker, Member of Parliament for the City of London 1832-42. He retired from Parliament to devote himself to historical work and wrote the *History of Greece* and *Aristotle*. He lived and died at 12 SAVILE ROW, Regent Street [3B 60c].

Guildhall [4B 64] The town hall of the City of London, built in about 1425, replacing a nearby earlier one. The hall, used for such events as the Lord Mayor's banquets and municipal meetings, was damaged in the fire of 1666, and again by incendiary bombs in 1940. The hall was formerly used for important trials including those of Anne Askew, a

Guildhall.

Protestant martyr burnt in Smithfield in 1546, Henry Howard, Earl of Surrey, executed on Tower Hill, 1547, and Archbishop Cranmer, found not guilty of high treason in 1554, The Guildhall houses a library, and an art gallery. The Guildhall museum is at present housed in GILLET HOUSE, Basinghall Street and contains relics of Roman and Medieval London.

Gunnersbury House, Acton [4C 56] In 1761 it was purchased for Princess Amelia, daughter of George II, for her summer residence. Later the estate was acquired by the Rothschild family who in 1926 sold it to the four local boroughs. The fine park contains two Regency houses (one of them is now a museum) and a temple.

Guns and Diamonds HATTON GARDEN [1B 61a], the headquarters of the diamond merchants, is named after Sir Christopher Hatton (1540-91), Lord Chancellor and dancing instructor to Elizabeth I. In 1884 an American, Hiram K. Maxim, invented the machine gun, which he designed, manufactured and later demonstrated in an underground range in Hatton House, Hatton Garden.

H

Ha-Ha Road, Woolwich Common [1D 83] A ha-ha is a sunken fence, a boundary that does not obscure the view. In the middle of the eighteenth century a landscape gardener, Mr Bridgman, built a low wall and fosse in KENSINGTON GARDENS at Kensington Palace which gave a better view of the park than the normal high wall. The name 'ha-ha' probably expresses the surprise felt at finding a ditch where there appears to be nothing.

Haldane, Lord Richard (1856-1928) Member of Parliament, lawyer, philosopher, minister of war 1905-12, lord chancellor. Author of *A Life of Adam Smith* and *Human Experience*. He lived at 28 QUEEN ANNE'S GATE, St James's Park [2D 62d].

Hallam, Henry (1777-1859) Historian. Educated at Eton. He is most famous for his '*The Constitutional History of England*' and '*A View of the State of Europe during the Middle Ages*'. He lived at 67 WIMPOLE STREET, W.1 [2A 60c].

Hamilton, Lady Emma (1761-1815) In 1778 she came to London to work as a nursemaid. In 1791 she was married at ST GEORGE'S, HANOVER SQUARE, to Sir William Hamilton, British ambassador to Naples. In 1798 she formed a liaison with Lord Nelson which lasted until his death. After the death of her husband, she served a term of imprisonment for debt. She lived

1803-6 at 11 CLARGES STREET, Piccadilly [4A 60c]. (The house was demolished in 1966.)

Hamilton Place, Hyde Park Corner [3C 60] Opened in June 1871 and thought to be named after Colonel James Hamilton, ranger of Hyde Park and friend of Charles II, who was killed fighting the Dutch in 1673.

Hammersmith From the middle of the seventeenth century until the late nineteenth century Hammersmith was noted for its market gardens, which supplied fruit and vegetables to Londoners.

Hand Court, High Holborn [2A 61a] Thought to have derived its name from a nearby tavern, The Hand in Hand. In former times, the sign of the Hand in Hand, which was very popular in this area, was displayed by a number of marriage brokers and taverns.

Hangman's Corner On Sundays many artists hang paintings for sale on the railings of Hyde Park along the Bayswater Road [3E 60b]. Because the gallows of Tyburn stood nearby, at Marble Arch, the corner is known as Hangman's Corner.

Hanway, Jonas (1712-1786) The man who introduced the umbrella to this country. He was a social reformer who fought for improved roads in London, the protection of boys working for chimney sweeps and better treatment for pauper children. He was part founder of the Magdalen Hospital for unmarried women, which stood for almost a hundred years in the Blackfriars Road. Buried in St Mary's parish church, Hanwell. HANWAY STREET, Oxford Street [2D 60d], commemorates his name.

Hardy, Thomas (1840-1928) Poet and novelist. He

was born in Dorset and originally trained as an architect. His novels include *Far from the Madding Crowd*, *Tess of the D'Urbervilles* and *Jude the Obscure*. He lived 1878-81 at 172 Trinity Road, Wandsworth Common [1A 92]. Buried in Westminster Abbey.

Harley-Portland Wedding St Peter's, Vere Street, Oxford Street [3A 60c], formerly called Marylebone Chapel, was built in 1724 for Edward Mortimer Harley, second Earl of Oxford, from designs by James Gibbs, the architect of St Martin-in-the-Fields (*see main entry*). Ten years later, in the same church, his daughter Margaret married William, the second Duke of Portland. Duchess Street and Margaret Street, Regent Street commemorate her.

Harvard University John Harvard (1607-38) Born in Borough High Street, baptized in Southwark Cathedral, where his father was churchwarden, and educated at St Saviour's Grammar School. He settled in Massachusetts and bequeathed part of his estate and all his books to the educational institution in Massachusetts which was named Harvard University after him. In 1907 the Harvard Chapel, Southwark Cathedral (*see main entry*), was rebuilt in his memory and a memorial window added.

Haydon, Benjamin (1786-1846) Artist. He was a student of the Royal Academy and his best-known paintings are 'Christ's Entry into Jerusalem' and 'The Raising of Lazarus'. He is also remembered for his autobiography and journals. Desperately in debt, he committed suicide. He lived at 1 Rossmore Road, Lisson Grove [4B 44]. Buried in St Mary's parish church, Paddington Green.

Haymarket, Piccadilly Circus [4D 60d] Now the home of two theatres and two cinemas, but originally it really was a hay market. During the reign of William III, traders were allowed to sell their hay and straw free of toll, but in 1692, when the streets in and around the market were paved, a levy had to be paid according to the loads on the carts. In 1830 the market was moved to Cumberland Market, off ALBANY STREET, Regent's Park.

Hazlitt, William (1778-1830) Writer who has been called the critic of critics. His works include *Characters of Shakespeare's Plays*, *Lectures on the English Poets* and *The Spirit of the Age*. In 1829 he lived at 4 BOUVERIE STREET, Fleet Street [3B 61a]. He died at 6 FRITH STREET, Soho [3D 60d], and is buried in ST ANNE'S, DEAN STREET, Soho.

Head and Heart Because the CITY is the centre of commercial transactions (Bank of England, Stock Exchange, etc.), it is known as the heart of the metropolis. WESTMINSTER, which contains the Queen's residence and Parliament and controls the political affairs of the nation, is called its head.

Heads and Tails Frances, Duchess of Richmond (*d.*1702), who posed for the original Britannia on our old copper coins, lived at 15 ST JAMES'S SQUARE, Pall Mall [4C 60c]. In WESTMINSTER ABBEY MUSEUM, there is a wax model of her, with a preserved parrot to keep her company which is thought to be the oldest stuffed parrot in the country.

Heart Transplant On 3 May 1968 a team of eighteen doctors and nurses under Dr Ross carried out England's first heart transplant at the NATIONAL HEART HOSPITAL, WESTMORELAND STREET, Marylebone [2A 60c]. The patient, forty-five year old Frederick West, survived until 17 June.

Herbert, Sidney (1810-61) Statesman. Born at Richmond. He entered Parliament in 1832 and was war minister in 1852-5. He was responsible for sending his friend, Florence Nightingale (*see main entry*), to the Crimea. In 1860 he was appointed Lord Herbert of Lea. The ROYAL HERBERT MILITARY HOSPITAL, BLACKHEATH, built soon after his death, was, at the suggestion of Florence Nightingale, named after him. Monument in WATERLOO PLACE, Pall Mall [4D 60d].

Highest The HILTON HOTEL, PARK LANE [3E 60b], opened in 1963, has twenty-eight floors and 512 bedrooms and is 327 ft high; it is the tallest hotel in London.

The WHITESTONE POND, HAMPSTEAD [4A 28], is 443ft above sea-level; it is the highest point in London.

The POST OFFICE TOWER in CLEVELAND STREET [1C 60c], completed in 1965, is 620ft high; it is the highest tower in London.

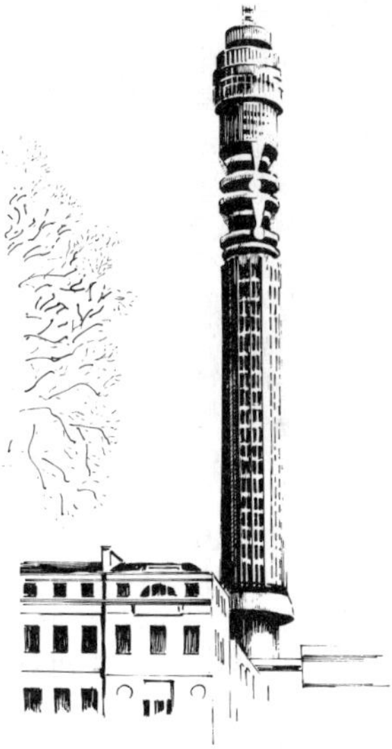

The Post Office Tower. At the top of this tower is a revolving restaurant which can provide spectacular views of London.

Highgate Hill [3D 29] Part of the old road from Islington to Highgate, it takes its name from the high gate on the hill which was the toll gate of the Bishop of London. At the foot of the hill is the WHITTINGTON STONE which in 1821 was placed on the spot where Richard Whittington (*see main entry*), Lord Mayor of London, is reputed to have heard Bow Bells peal 'Turn again, Whittington'.

Highwayman Jack Sheppard (1702-24), born in WHITE'S ROW, Commercial Street [2B 61c], was an apprentice carpenter, but turned highwayman. He was captured, sentenced to death and committed to NEWGATE PRISON, from which he escaped. Recaptured, he was kept chained in the prison. Again, he escaped and was caught. On a November day he was hanged at TYBURN. His ashes were scattered in the churchyard of ST MARTIN-IN-THE-FIELDS, Trafalgar Square.

Hogarth, William (1697-1764) Painter and engraver. Born in BARTHOLOMEW CLOSE [2D 61b], baptized in ST BARTHOLOMEW'S CHURCH, Smithfield and married at ST. JAMES', PADDINGTON GREEN now St Mary's [1B 60a]. He was instrumental in 1735 in getting a law through protecting the copyright of engravers. His best-known works are the *Harlot's Progress*, the *Rake's Progress* and *Marriage à la Mode*. He lived at 30 LEICESTER SQUARE [3D 60d], and, from 1749 until his death, at HOGARTH HOUSE (now a National Trust House) Hogarth Lane, Chiswick [1F 73]. Buried in St NICHOLAS'S CHURCH, CHISWICK MALL [1A 74].

Holloway Prison This ladies' prison in PARKHURST ROAD, Holloway [1F 45], known to the inmates as 'the castle', was built in 1850 on land originally purchased for a cemetery. The central tower is said to be designed to the shape of Caesar's camp on Warwick Castle.

Holywell Lane, Shoreditch High Street [1A 61c] Said to occupy the site of the holy well of St Agnes Le Clare, which was fed from an underground stream which flowed from Stoke Newington.

Homosexual Dance On 22 December 1970 a crowd of men and women attended a public dance at the KENSINGTON TOWN HALL organized by the homosexual movement, the Gay Liberation Front. All members attending were given a copy of the movement's journal, *Come Together*. This was the first public social event organized for homosexuals.

Honor Oak, near Dulwich [1F 95] Queen Elizabeth I once had her lunch in the shade of an oak tree, which was then called 'the oak of honour' and later Honor Oak. The original tree that shaded the queen was destroyed by a storm, but another oak was planted in its place.

Hood, Thomas (1799-1845) Poet. Born in POULTRY, City [3E 61b]. At the age of twenty-two, he was appointed sub-editor of the *London Magazine*. His best-known works are 'The Song of the Shirt', 'Bridge of Sighs' and 'I Remember, I Remember'. He lived at 17 ELM TREE ROAD, St John's Wood [4A 44]. Buried in KENSAL GREEN CEMETERY.

Hopton Street, Southwark [4C 61a] Named after Charles Hopton who in 1752 built a row of almshouses for twenty-eight distressed house-keepers. The houses were damaged by bombs in the Second World War, but have since been restored.

Horse Bus and Tram In July 1829 George Shillibeer ran the first of London's horse-drawn buses, subsequently known as 'Shillibeers', from The Yorkshire Stingo, a tavern in the old Marylebone Road, via

City Road, to the Bank of England. The first horse tramways were built in 1861 by an American, Mr G. Train, who ran the service from Marble Arch to Porchester Terrace, Bayswater.

Horseferry Road, Millbank [3D 62d] Derives its name from an ancient horse-ferry that linked the PALACE OF WESTMINSTER (*see Houses of Parliament*) with LAMBETH PALACE (*see main entry*). The fees from the ferry were part of the income of the Archbishop of Canterbury, who held the manorial rights; in 1862, when the first Lambeth Bridge was built, the See was awarded £2,200 compensation for lost revenue.

Houndsditch, Bishopsgate [2A 61c] Used to be outside the city walls and takes its name from an old moat in which the bodies of dead dogs floated.

Houses of Parliament [2E 62d] Officially called the Palace of Westminster, the Houses of Parliament stand on the site of the old royal PALACE OF WESTMINSTER. This palace was occupied by Edward the Confessor (r. 1042-66) and was the sovereign's chief London

The Houses of Parliament, viewed from across the Thames.

residence until Henry VIII moved to the nearby Whitehall Palace in 1529 after fire had damaged Westminster Palace. WESTMINSTER HALL was built by William Rufus in 1097-9 and rebuilt by Richard II in 1399 after a fire. In 1834 Westminster Palace was almost completely destroyed by yet another fire, although Westminster Hall fortunately survived. The present neo-Gothic Houses of Parliament were built 1840-52 from designs by Sir Charles Barry. During the Second World War they were bombed on no less than fourteen occasions; the House of Commons was destroyed and rebuilt 1948-50. When the House of Commons is in session there is a flag on the Victoria Tower by day and a light on the Clock Tower by night.

Howard League John Howard (1726-90), philanthropist and prison reformer, born in Lower Clapton, in 1773 was appointed high sheriff for Bedford County and went on a tour of English prisons. His accounts of his findings brought many reforms. The school in LAURA PLACE, Clapton [1F 47], and the Howard League for Penal Reform, founded in 1834, commemorate his name. He lived at 23 GREAT ORMOND STREET, Bloomsbury [1F 60d]. Buried in ST PAUL'S CATHEDRAL.

Hungarian Patriot Lajos Kossuth (1802-94), leader of the Hungarian liberals, demanded his country's independence from Austria. He raised an army, but in August 1849 the Hungarians were defeated by Austrian and Russian troops and Kossuth fled to Turkey. In 1852 he came to England, where he remained for ten years, living at 39 CHEPSTOW VILLAS, Portobello Road [2E 59].

Hunt, Leigh (1784-1859) Poet and essayist. Educated at Christ's Hospital. Editor of *The Examiner*. He served a two-year prison sentence for an attack on the Prince Regent. His best-known works are *The Story of Rimini* and 'Abou Ben Adhem and the Angel'. He lived at 22 UPPER CHEYNE ROW, Chelsea [1B 76], and died in poverty in Putney. Buried in KENSAL GREEN CEMETERY.

Hunt, William Holman (1827-1910) English Pre-Raphaelite painter. His best-known works are 'The Light of the World' and 'The Scapegoat'. He lived and died at 18 MELBURY ROAD, High Street, Kensington [3E 59].

Hunter, John (1728-93) Surgeon and physiologist. He discovered the circulation in the human placenta, and lectured in surgery. His anatomical collections were acquired by the nation and are housed in the Royal College of Surgeons, Lincoln's Inn Fields. He lived at 31 GOLDEN SQUARE, Soho (*see main entry*). He was house surgeon to ST GEORGE'S HOSPITAL, HYDE PARK CORNER, where he died. Monument in LEICESTER SQUARE. Buried in WESTMINSTER ABBEY.

Hyde Park [4D 60b] The Manor of Hyde was the property of Westminster Abbey from the Norman Conquest until 1536. Henry VIII confiscated it and made it into a hunting forest, and in 1635, Charles I opened it to the public. Hyde Park has an area of 350 acres and merges into KENSINGTON GARDENS to the west. ROTTON ROW, the sandy track on the south side of the park was perhaps originally called 'Route Du Roi', the king's road, and is reserved for horse-riding, while the SERPENTINE (*see main entry*) offers rowing, sailing and bathing.

Hydrogen at Clapham Common Henry Cavendish (1731-1810), scientist, known as the Newton of chemistry, in 1766 discovered hydrogen. He also experimented on electricity and the density of the earth. He carried out his experiments in CAVENDISH ROAD, Clapham Common South Side [4D 77], which commemorates his name. He lived at 11 BEDFORD SQUARE, Bloomsbury [2D 60d].

I

Imperial War Museum, Lambeth Road [3F 62d] The museum, which covers all aspects of war since 1914, contains a gallery of paintings by official war artists and trophies, relics and objects associated with the two world wars. From 1815 to 1930 the building housed the Bethlehem Hospital (known as Bedlam), the first hospital for the insane which was originally founded in 1246 where Liverpool Street now is and from 1676 to 1815 occupied a site in London Wall. In 1930 the hospital moved from Lambeth Road to Kent and the museum took over the buildings.

Irish Club At 82 Eaton Square, Belgravia [3F 62b]. The club, opened in 1950, is non-political and open to all men and women who are Irish by birth, descent or nationality, and to their children.

Irish Flag The flag that was hoisted over the General Post Office in Dublin during the Easter Rising in 1916 was in the custody of the Imperial War Museum, Lambeth, Rd., until 1966, when it was returned to Eire.

Irving, Sir Henry (1838-1905) Actor. He became famous with his performances in *The Bells* and *Hamlet* at the Lyceum Theatre. In 1878 he became manager of the Lyceum with Ellen Terry as his leading lady. In 1895 he was knighted, the first actor ever to be so honoured. He lived 1872-99 at the corner of Grafton Street and New Bond Street [4B 60c]. Monument at the corner of IRVING STREET and Charing Cross Road [4D 60d]. Buried in WESTMINSTER ABBEY.

Italian Composer Muzio Clementi (1752-1832), born in Rome, played in London in 1770 and later settled here. From 1776-80 he was conductor at the Royal Italian Opera House. His works include many sonatas, symphonies, overtures and the *Gradus ad Parnassum*. He lived at 128 KENSINGTON CHURCH STREET [2F 59].

Italian Patriot Giuseppe Mazzini (1805-72) was one of the most important figures in the unification of Italy and the founder of the 'Young Italy' revolutionary movement. Exiled from Italy, he came twice to London in 1837 and again in 1850 and he carried on his political work here. He lived at 10 LAYSTALL STREET, Clerkenwell [1A 61a], 183 NORTH GOWER STREET, Euston [4E 45], and 5 HATTON GARDEN [1B 61a].

James II (1633-1701) Born in ST JAMES'S PALACE (*see main entry*), son of Charles I. In 1660, he commanded the British fleet against the Dutch and in 1685 he succeeded Charles II. He was a Roman Catholic convert whose arbitrary rule and favouring of Catholics produced a reaction against him. Unable to defend the Crown against William of Orange, his son-in-law, James fled the country and died in exile. Statue in TRAFALGAR SQUARE.

James, Henry (1843-1916) Novelist. He was born in New York, but spent most of his life in Europe and became a naturalized British subject in 1915. His most famous works are *Portrait of a Lady*, *The Bostonians*, *The Wings of a Dove* and *The Turn of the Screw*. He lived 1886-1902 on the site of Hale House, DE VERE GARDENS, Kensington [3F 59].

Jellicoe, John Rushworth, first Earl (1859-1935) Commander-in-chief of the Grand Fleet 1914-6, he fought the battle of Jutland, became admiral of the fleet in 1919 and Governor-General of New Zealand 1920-4. Monument in TRAFALGAR SQUARE. Buried in ST PAUL'S CATHEDRAL.

Jerry-Built The BRUNSWICK THEATRE, WELLCLOSE SQUARE, Stepney [4C 61c], was opened on 25 February 1828. Only four days later, on 29 February, the entire structure collapsed, killing twelve people.

Jewish Justice There is a drinking fountain bearing a bronze bust of Edward VII opposite the London Hospital in the Whitechapel Road [2C 61c]. The monument, erected in 1911 with money raised by the Jewish community of East London, is dedicated to liberty and justice.

Jubilee Place, King's Road, Chelsea [4D 62b] Built in about 1810 to commemorate George III's jubilee (he reigned 1760-1820).

Judd Street, Euston Road [4F 45] Commemorates Sir Andrew Judd who was Lord Mayor of London in 1551 and built a grammar school in Tonbridge, Kent, his native town, in 1553. Buried in ST HELEN'S CHURCH, BISHOPSGATE (*see City Abbey*).

Jury Exemption The following are exempt from serving on juries in the City of London: income-tax Commissioners, Jewish ministers, Roman Catholic priests, Members of Parliament, peers, prison officers and servants of the Queen's Household.

K

Keats, John (1795-1821) Poet. Born at 85 MOORGATE, City, and baptized at ST BOTOLPH'S, BISHOPSGATE. He qualified in surgery but abandoned it for poetry. His works include 'Ode to a Nightingale', 'Endymion' and 'The Eve of St Agnes'. He lived 1817-20 at KEATS HOUSE (then known as Wentworth Place), Keats Grove, Hampstead [1B 44]. The house is now a National Trust house and contains a Keats museum. He died of consumption in Rome.

Kennington Originally a village in the precincts of Lambeth. The royal residence of the Black Prince (1330-76), eldest son of Edward III, stood on or near BLACK PRINCE ROAD, Lambeth [4F 62d].

Kensal Green Cemetery, Harrow Road [4C 42] The first large cemetery to be built in the precincts of London—before its construction in 1832 most burials took place in churchyards. Among the many notables buried here are the tight-rope walker Blondin (*see main entry*) and the writers Wilkie Collins (*see Detective Novelist*) and W. M. Thackeray (*see main entry*).

Kensington In 1901 Queen Victoria, who was born in KENSINGTON PALACE (*see London Museum*), granted Kensington the Royal Charter, thus making it the Royal Borough of Kensington. It is now incorporated into the Borough of Chelsea.

Kensington Fire Station In Old Court Place, off High Street Kensington [3F 59]. This was the last of London's fire brigades to use horse-drawn fire appliances. The last occasion was in December 1921.

Kent Terrace, Regent's Park [4B 44] Named after Edward Augustus, Duke of Kent (1767-1820), fourth son of George III and father of Queen Victoria. In 1799 he was created commander in North America and three years later was appointed Governor of Gibraltar. Statue in PARK CRESCENT, Marylebone Road [1A 60c].

Kilburn The Kilburn Wells stood at or near the present junction of KILBURN HIGH ROAD and BELSIZE ROAD [3F 43], The spot, which had some beautiful gardens and was noted for its pure water, became a place of entertainment for music and dancing on the site of the former Abbey of Kilburn.

King Maker WARWICK LANE, Newgate Street [3C 61a], commemorates Richard Neville, Earl of Warwick (1428-71), whose town house stood near here. He was called the king maker because in 1461 he was responsible for placing Edward IV on the throne. Nine years later he restored Henry VI, who within a few months was found murdered in the Tower. The Earl of Warwick was killed by Edward in a battle at Barnet.

King's Cross [4F 45] Until 1830 it was known as Battle Bridge (*see Boadicea*), and was renamed because of a statue of George IV that was erected at the point where the six streets converged. The monument had eight doric columns 60ft high and was surmounted by a statue of the king 11ft high. It was removed in 1845.

Kipling, Rudyard (1865-1936) Poet and author. Born in Bombay. He was awarded the Nobel Prize for literature in 1907. Author of such works as *Stalky and Co.*, the *Jungle Books*, *Kim* and the *Just So Stories* and the poems 'If' and 'Gunga Din'. He lived 1889-91 at 43 VILLIERS STREET, Strand [4E 60d]. Buried in WESTMINSTER ABBEY.

Knightsbridge [2D 62b] Legend has it that two knights leaving London to fight in a holy war had a quarrel. They fought on the bridge which spanned the bourn, or stream (hence BOURNE STREET near Sloane Square). Both were killed and forever more the place was called the Knightsbridge.

L

Labour Constituencies In the 1892 general election Keir Hardy won the seat for West Ham and John Burns won the seat for Battersea. They thus became the first Labour MPs.

Ladbroke Road, Notting Hill [2E 59] Built on part of the site of the Hippodrome, a race-course that opened in 1837 and closed in 1841. Ladbroke Road, Ladbroke Grove, etc. are named after Richard Ladbroke, the lease holder and son of a Lord Mayor of London.

Ladies All Tyburn Road was in 1729 renamed Oxford Street [3F 60b]. This street, almost a mile in length and one of the finest and most spectacular shopping streets in the world, was once known as the 'ladies' mile'. The Achilles Statue, a naked statue at Hyde Park Corner [3C 60] is called the 'ladies' trophy' because it was erected in 1822 to the Duke of Wellington and his companions in arms 'by their countrywomen'. It was cast from cannons taken in the victories at Salamanca, Vittoria, Toulouse and Waterloo.

Lady Boxing Promoter In 1782 the Rev. Rowland built the Surrey Chapel in the Blackfriars Road on the corner of Union Street [1C 63a] and in 1785 London's first Sunday school opened there. In 1910 it became a centre for boxing known as the Ring, Blackfriars. A Mrs Burge who became its owner after the death of her husband promoted the fights there until 1940 when it was bombed. She was thus the first woman boxing promoter.

Lamb, Charles (1775-1834) Essayist and critic. Born in the Inner Temple, Strand and educated at Christ's Hospital. He spent his life looking after his sister, Mary, after she had killed their mother in a fit of insanity in 1796. His works include the *Essays of Elia* and the *Tales from Shakespeare*, written in collaboration with Mary. They lived 1823-7 at 64 DUNCAN TERRACE, Islington [4B 46], and are both buried in the churchyard of ALL SAINTS, EDMONTON.

Lambeth Palace [3F 62d] Occupies the site of a Saxon manor given by William the Conqueror to the Benedictine monks of Rochester. The palace, the London residence of the Archbishops of Canterbury, was built by Archbishop Langton (1207-28). In 1381 Wat Tyler's rebels on their march to London attacked the palace. The residential section was added 1829-33. In 1941 the palace sustained heavy bomb damage, but has been restored.

Lambeth Walk [3A 63a] It was in December 1937, at the Victoria Palace, that Lupino Lane popularized this little street off the Lambeth Road when he sang and danced the 'Lambeth Walk' in his new musical show *Me and My Girl.*

Lamb's Conduit Street, Bloomsbury [1F 60d] Commemorates the name of William Lamb, a clothworker who built a conduit to supply the district with water. At Sutton Valence in Kent, the place of his birth he built almshouses and a school, and at MONKWELL STREET, City [2E 61b], he erected a number of almshouses.

Lancaster House, Stable Yard [1C 62c] Built originally for the son of George III, the Duke of York and Albany, who died in 1827 just before its completion. The unfinished mansion was taken over by the Marquis of Stafford (later Duke of Sutherland), and completed by Robert Smirke and Charles Barry. In 1912 the house was bought by the first Lord Leverhume (the soap manufacturer), who renamed it Lancaster House and presented it to the nation. It housed the London Museum (*see main entry*) until 1941 when the museum was moved to Kensington Palace. Lancaster House is now used for government conferences and hospitality.

Largest Buildings The SHELL CENTRE on the South Bank, York Road, Waterloo [1A 63a], was opened in October 1962. It is twenty-four storeys high and its viewing gallery is 317ft above ground level. It is said to be the largest office in Europe.
DOLPHIN SQUARE, Westminster [1E 77], a block of flats completed in 1937 has over 1200 flats, a squash court, an arcade of shops, a restaurant and a swimming pool. It is the largest block of flats in Britain.

Law, Andrew Bonar (1858-1923) Born in Canada, Tory Member of Parliament. He was prime minister from 1922-3, but was forced to retire through ill health. He lived at 24 ONSLOW GARDENS, South Kensington [4B 62a], and is buried in WESTMINSTER ABBEY.

Law Courts, Strand [3A 61a] From the middle of the thirteenth century until 1882, the Supreme Courts of Justice were convened at Westminster Hall, which was part of the Royal Palace of Westminster (*see Houses of Parliament*). It was there that Richard II was deposed in 1399 and that Charles I stood trial in 1649. The Royal Courts of Justice (as they are properly called) in the Strand were built 1874-82 from designs by G. E. Street who died before the work's completion. It was finished by his son A. E. Street and Sir Arthur Blomfield.

Lawrence of Arabia Thomas Edward Lawrence (1888-1935), soldier, during the First World War organized an Arab revolt against the Turks, and was himself a brilliant guerrilla leader. His book *The Seven Pillars of Wisdom* gives an account of the revolt. He later changed his name to Ross to avoid publicity and joined the RAF. He was killed in a motor-cycle accident. He lived at 14 BARTON STREET, Westminster [2E 62d].

Law Society, Chancery Lane [2A 61a] Founded in June 1825 and called The Law Institution. In 1827 the

The Law Courts, in the Strand. More properly called The Royal Courts of Justice.

Society acquired its present site and in 1831 received the first of its five Royal Charters. The Society, which is the headquarters for solicitors, has over 20,000 members and a library of over 60,000 volumes.

Laycock Street, Highbury Corner [2A 46] Named after a Mr Laycock (*d.* 1834) who owned a number of small farms near here and supplied sheds for cattle on their way to SMITHFIELD MARKET.

Leadenhall Market [3F 61b] London's chief poultry market, in the City, stands on the site of an old manor with a leaded roof, an unusual feature in olden times which gave the market its name. The manor, once the property of Sir Richard Whittington (*see main entry*), was acquired by the Corporation of London in about 1411. The present market was rebuilt in 1881.

Lear, Edward (1812-88) Humorist and artist. He painted landscapes of Italy, Greece, Egypt and India and exhibited regularly at the Royal Academy. He wrote the *Book of Nonsense* and is noted for his limericks. He lived at 30 SEYMOUR STREET, Marble Arch [3D 60b].

Leathersellers The Worshipful Company of Leathersellers was granted the Charter of Incorporation in 1444. The Company has had six halls, including the present one in ST HELEN'S PLACE, Bishopsgate [2A 61c], which was built in 1959. The Leathersellers' Company are the trustees of the Colfe Foundation at Lewisham and have endowed almshouses at Barnet.

Left-Handed In June 1969 the first ever left-handed shop opened at 65 BEAK STREET, Soho [3C 60c]. Its owner, William Gruby, soon discovered that the articles most in demand were left-handed pens, potato-peelers and scissors.

Legendary Railway Station Legend has it that Queen Boadicea (*see main entry*) of the Iceni lies under the site of Platform 10 at KING'S CROSS STATION [4F 45]. The clock which adorned the Crystal Palace during the 1851 Exhibition in Hyde Park is now in the tower of this station.

Leicester Square [3D 60d] Derives its name from Leicester House, built 1632-6 for Robert Sidney, Earl of Leicester, on land that was a favourite resort for duellists. The mansion was later acquired by George II, as Prince of Wales, and was demolished in 1790. The square, laid out 1665, was originally known as Leicester Fields until 1678 when it became Leicester Square. In 1870 it was bought by Albert Grant (later Baron Grant), who had the gardens laid out in their present form and donated them to the public. The square contains a statue of Shakespeare in the centre and busts of Newton, Reynolds, Hogarth and Hunter (*see main entries*), who all lived in or near the square, at the corners. It is surrounded by some of London's most famous West End cinemas.

Leighton House, 12 Holland Park Road, Kensington [3E 59] Built in 1866 for Lord Leighton (1830-96), the painter, who lived there until his death. In 1896 his sisters gave the house as a gift to the nation and thirty years later it was transferred to the care of Kensington Borough Council. Drawings and paintings by Lord Leighton and others can be seen in the house which is now a centre for Victorian studies. Lord Leighton is buried in the crypt of ST PAUL'S CATHEDRAL.

Leman Street, Aldgate East [3C 61c] Built in about 1710 by Sir William Leman on the site of Goodman's Fields, a farm belonging to the Abbey of the nuns of St Clare. ALIE STREET, MANSELL STREET and PRESCOT

STREET are thought to be named after relatives of Sir William. Prescot Street and GOODMAN STREET were among the first streets in London to have their houses numbered.

Lenin Pen-name of Vladimir Ilyich Ulanovitch (1870-1924), Russian statesman. Expelled from Kazan University for his political activities, he was imprisoned and banished to Siberia for organizing trade unions. Forced to leave Russia in 1905, he visited London several times and eventually settled in Switzerland in 1914. In 1917 he returned to Russia and led the Bolshevik Revolution. In 1905 he lived at 16 PERCY CIRCUS, King's Cross [4A 46]. He used to print the newspaper *Iskra*, for distribution in Russia, at 37-8 CLERKENWELL GREEN, Clerkenwell [1C 61a].

Lighthouses The Corporation of Trinity House, an ancient 'guild, fraternity and brotherhood', was founded in Deptford in the reign of Henry VIII, who granted it its first charter. The present TRINITY HOUSE near the TOWER [4B 61c] was built in 1795 and damaged during the blitz but restored in 1953. It controls all lighthouses and buoys round the shores of England and Wales and works in collaboration with the Royal Navy. It is also responsible for granting licences to the Thames pilots and escorting the royal yacht in home waters.

Limehouse, in the borough of Tower Hamlets [1A 64], was once noted for its lime-kilns. LIME STREET, near Fenchurch Street in the City [3F 61b], is so called either because it was once a market of lime, or because a number of lime trees grew there.

Lincoln, Abraham (1809-65) Sixteenth president of the USA. He was self-educated, but qualified and practised as a lawyer. He joined the Republican party in 1856, was elected president in 1860 and re-elected in 1864. He was an opponent of slavery, and the Civil War between north and south took place during his presidency. He was assassinated a few days after the end of the war. Statue in PARLIAMENT SQUARE.

Lincoln's Inn Fields, Kingsway [2F 60d] One of London's largest squares laid out by Inigo Jones early in the seventeenth century. The Fields became a noted resort for duellists and here in 1683 Lord William Russell, who was implicated in the Rye House plot was executed. Lincoln's Inn, one of the four great Inns of Court, perhaps commemorates the name of Henry De Lacey, third earl of Lincoln (*d.*1311), whose residence stood nearby. The Inn of Court is known to have been on its present site since 1422 when records commenced. Former famous associates of the Inn include Sir Thomas More, Cardinal Newman, Disraeli and Gladstone.

'Little America' Ever since John Adams, later second president of the USA, lived 1785-8 at 9 GROSVENOR SQUARE, Mayfair [3F 60b], it has been associated with the USA. During the Second World War almost every building in the square was requisitioned for the American armed forces and it soon became known as 'Little America'. It now contains the American Embassy.

'Little Britain', Aldersgate Street [2D 61b] So called either because a Robert Le Bretoun was the owner of the property, or because the Earls of Brittany had a residence here.

'Little Moscow' Holly Lodge Estate in SWAINS LANE, Highgate [3D 29] was until recently known as 'Little Moscow'. This estate was the home of several members of the Soviet diplomatic staff and their families until September 1971, when a number of them were accused of spying and expelled from the country.

Lombard Street, Mansion House [3F 61b] derives its name from the Lombards, merchants of Genoa, Florence and Venice who settled here in the thirteenth century and established themselves as money lenders, bankers and pawnbrokers. They are credited with introducing the term L.S.D. which originally stood for Libri, Solidi, and Denarii. They were the first in this country to set up as pawnbrokers and the sign of the Three Golden Balls represents three golden pills which they adopted from the Medicis family who once specialised in medicine.

London Bridge [4F 61b] It is possible that a bridge stood just east of the present one as early as AD 50, but the first known one was a timber bridge built 973-5. The first stone bridge was opened in 1209 and was until 1749 the only one over the Thames. It was demolished in 1832 after the completion of the second one, built by the Rennie family and opened on 1 August 1832 by William IV. This bridge was bought by the Americans in 1968 (*see America's London Bridge*) and its modern replacement is designed by Harold King and Charles Brown. Stones of the original bridge can be seen in the churchyard at ST MAGNUS THE MARTYR, MONUMENT. The coat of arms that surmounted the southern gateway of the original bridge is now attached to the façade of the King's Head, NEWCOMEN STREET, Borough High St [1E 63b].

London Lights In 1415 London was for the first time illuminated by means of lanterns. Gas lighting was introduced in 1807 and electricity in 1878, on the VICTORIA EMBANKMENT [4F 60d]. ST MARTIN-IN-THE-FIELDS, TRAFALGAR SQUARE (*see main entry*) was in

1808 the first church to install gas, and in 1888 the first to install electricity.

London Museum, Kensington Palace [3F 59] Occupies the basement and ground floor of Kensington Palace and displays such items as prehistoric implements, Saxon brooches, toys and dolls' houses and clothing from the Tudor Period onward. It was the sovereign's private residence until 1760. It was here, at Kensington Palace that Queen Victoria was born and later told that she was to be Queen of England.

London Stone A piece of stone first mentioned in the tenth century and thought to be the landmark from which the Romans measured distances. Before being placed in its present position, set into the wall of the Bank of China opposite CANNON STREET STATION [3E 61b], it was attached to the wall of the now demolished St Swithin's church which stood on this site.

Long Acre, Covent Garden [3E 60d] Formerly called 'Seven Acres', the street takes its name from a strip of land owned by the Abbot of Westminster which bordered the garden of the convent and was used as a pathway. The street was in the past noted for its carriage-builders. Oliver Cromwell (*see main entry*) and John Dryden (*see Dryden Street*) were once residents of the street.

Lord Mayor of London Henry Fitz-Aylwin, London's first mayor, took office in 1189 and in 1215 King John decreed that the mayor was to be elected annually. Nowadays the mayor is chosen on 29 September and the Lord Mayor's Show takes place on the second Saturday in November. The Lord Mayor, besides being a magistrate and Admiral of the Port of London, has precedence over every subject in the city except the reigning monarch.

Lottery The earliest recorded lottery in England took place in January 1569 at the west door of the old St Paul's Cathedral. The profits from this lottery, in which shares were sold at ten shillings, went to the upkeep of harbours and other public works.

Lowndes Square, Knightsbridge [2E 62b] Built on the site of a coppice which was used to supply the Abbot and Convent of Westminster with wood for fuel. The square, laid out in 1838 by Thomas Cubitt (*see main entry*), takes its name from the ground landlord, a Mr Lowndes of Bury in Buckinghamshire.

Lyell, Sir Charles (1797-1875) Geologist, Professor of Geology at King's College, Strand, President of the Geological Society 1835-6 and 1849-50, author of *Principles of Geology* and *The Antiquity of Man*. He lived and died at 73 HARLEY STREET, Marylebone [1A 60c].

M

Macklin, Charles [1699-1797] Irish-born actor and playwright. He gained fame as a Shakespearean actor and acted mainly at the Drury Lane Theatre. His own plays include *Love a la Mode* and *The Man of the World.* Buried in St Paul's, Covent Garden (*see Actors' Church*). Macklin Street, off Drury Lane [2E 60d], commemorates his name.

Maida Vale [3F 43] Commemorates the victory of the Battle of Maida in Calabria, Italy, in 1806, when Sir John Stuart, who led the British forces, defeated the French.

Malone, Edmund (1741-1812) Irish author, critic and authority on Shakespeare. In 1778 he published *Attempt to Ascertain the Order in which the Plays of Shakespeare were Written.* He lived 1779-1812 at 40 Langham Street, Portland Place [2B 60c].

Mansfield, Katherine (1888-1923) New Zealand writer who lived most of her life in England. Famous for her volumes of short stories which include *In a German Pension*, *Bliss* and *The Garden Party*, She lived at 17 East Heath Road, Hampstead [4A 28].

Mansion House [3E 61b] The official residence of the Lord Mayor of London (*see main entry*) during his year in office, built in 1753 by George Dance the Elder (*see Dance*). In order to raise money to build this mansion, fines were imposed on those who refused to accept the office of sheriff. There is a story that a number of influential people were chosen because they could not accept the office. The first occupant was Sir Crisp Gascoigne, Lord Mayor in 1753.

Marble Arch [3E 60b] Designed in 1828 by John Nash, who modelled it on the Arch of Constantine in Rome and originally intended to be the main gateway to Buckingham Palace. However, it was found to be too narrow for the state coach, so in 1851 it was moved to its present site.

Markets The great wholesale markets – COVENT GARDEN, SMITHFIELD, LEADENHALL, BILLINGSGATE,

A Lavender Seller of many years ago whose market cry of 'Sweet Lavender' might be heard around any market.

SPITALFIELDS (*see main entries*) and the BOROUGH MARKET [1E 63b] – do most of their trade early in the morning, but there are more than a hundred street markets selling every kind of article – for example PETTICOAT LANE, Middlesex Street [2A 61c], Sunday mornings; PORTOBELLO ROAD, Notting Hill [1D 59], for antiques, Saturdays; BERWICK STREET, Soho [3C 60c]; LEATHER LANE, Holborn [1B 61a]; CAMDEN PASSAGE, Islington [3B 46].

Marlborough House, St James's Park [1C 62c] Built by Sir Christopher Wren 1709-11 for the first Duke of Marlborough (the victor of Blenheim) who lived there until he died in 1722. Queen Mary, wife of George V, lived here from 1936 until her death in 1953. In 1962 it was converted to a Commonwealth Conference Centre.

Marryat, Captain Frederick (1792-1848) Novelist who served with distinction as captain in the Royal Navy. He wrote a number of novels about sea-life including *Peter Simple* and *Mr Midshipman Easy* and such children's books as *The Children of the New Forest* and *Masterman Ready*. He lived at 3 SPANISH PLACE, north of Oxford Street [2F 60b].

Maryland, USA Baltimore, George Calvert, 1st Baron (1580-1632). Member of Parliament, Secretary of State, was also on the 1613 Committee sent out of Ireland to investigate complaints made by the Catholics. He established Ferryland, a small settlement in Newfoundland. Founded Maryland, USA, which is named in honour of Queen Henrietta Maria, but he died before he could obtain the Charter. Buried in ST. DUNSTANS-IN-THE-WEST, Fleet Street [3B 61a].

Maternity Hospital Queen Charlotte's Maternity Hospital has the distinction of being the first lying-in hospital in the country. Founded in 1739 with the title of the Queen's Lying-in Hospital in JERMYN STREET, Piccadilly, it moved in 1809 to MARYLEBONE ROAD and in 1940 to its present quarters in the GOLDHAWK ROAD, Hammersmith [4A 58].

Mathematical Inventor Charles Babbage (1791-1871), founder and secretary of the Astronomical Society and author of *Economy of Machinery*, devoted over thirty years of his life and a great deal of his income, to perfecting the calculating machine which he had invented. He lived from 1829 until his death at 1a DORSET STREET, Baker Street [2E 60b].

Mayfair Named after a May Fair which took place annually from the thirteenth century until 1809. CURZON STREET, TREBECK STREET and SHEPHERD MARKET [4A 60c] were built on the site of the old fair.

Mercury The figure that surmounts the tower on Royal London House, FINSBURY SQUARE, Moorgate [1F 61b], is the work of James Stevenson. The bronze figure, which exemplifies progress and prudence, was first exhibited at the Royal Academy in 1929.

Mermaid Theatre, Puddle Dock [3C 61a] Opened in 1959 by Sir Bernard Miles, the actor-manager. This was the City of London's first new theatre for three hundred years.

Messiah George Frederick Handel (1685-1759), German-born composer, in 1711 came to London for a short spell and returned a year later, becoming a naturalized Englishman in 1726. He was a governor of the FOUNDLING HOSPITAL (*see Coram's Fields*) where he trained the choir. He wrote a number of operas and oratorios (*see Oratorio*), the famous 'Water

Music' for George I, and the *Messiah*, composed at 25 BROOK STREET, Mayfair [3A 60c], where he lived and died. HANDEL STREET [4F 45], near Coram's Fields, commemorates his name. Buried in WESTMINSTER ABBEY.

Methodism John Wesley (1703-91), the founder of Methodism, was educated at Charterhouse School. He travelled around the country on horseback in order to preach and is said to have preached about 40,000 sermons. He also published twenty-three collections of hymns. He lived the last twelve years of his life and died at 47 CITY ROAD, Moorgate [4B 46], beside the chapel which he founded in 1778 and is buried in the churchyard. He was assisted in his work by his brother Charles (1707-88), who wrote some 6,500 hymns including 'Jesu, lover of my soul'. Charles Wesley lived and died on the site of a tavern near the junction of WHEATLEY STREET and WESTMORELAND STREET, Marylebone; nearby WESLEY STREET commemorates his name. Buried in the little churchyard of the now demolished Marylebone chapel on the north-west of High Street, Marylebone. Monument in WESTMINSTER ABBEY.

Meynell, Alice (1847-1922) Poet and essayist. Her works include *Preludes* and *The Rhythm of Life*. With her husband, she assisted the poet Francis Thompson, who was living in poverty. She lived at 47 PALACE COURT, Bayswater Road [2F 59], and is buried in KENSAL GREEN CEMETERY.

Mile End Road [1E 61d] Probably so called because it started a mile away from Aldgate or because it was a Roman encampment a mile long. It was the birthplace of the Salvation Army (*see Salvation Rink*) and there is a bust of William Booth, the founder, on the left of the road.

Milky Way To ensure that Londoners were well supplied with milk during the General Strike of 1926, the roadway inside HYDE PARK leading from Marble Arch to Victoria Gate was used as a milk depot. Here thousands of lorries stopped and unloaded the milk.

Mill, John Stuart (1806-73) Economist and philosopher. Born in PENTON STREET, Pentonville Road [3A 46], Radical Member of Parliament for Westminster 1865-8. His works include *On Liberty*, *Principles of Political Economy* and *On the Subjection of Women*. He lived 1836-50 at 18 KENSINGTON SQUARE, Kensington [3F 59]. Statue on VICTORIA EMBANKMENT [1E 62d].

Millais, Sir John Everett (1829-96) Artist and one of the founders of the Pre-Raphaelite brotherhood. He was very popular for such paintings as 'Bubbles' and 'The Boyhood of Raleigh'. He lived and died at 2 PALACE GATE, Kensington [2A 62a]. Buried in ST PAUL'S CATHEDRAL. Statue in the forecourt of the TATE GALLERY.

Millbank Penitentiary Erected 1813-6 on the site now occupied by the TATE GALLERY (*see main entry*). It housed 1,500 prisoners and was the largest prison in London at that period. It was closed in 1890 and demolished in 1893.

Millionaires' Row KENSINGTON PALACE GARDENS [2F 59], built in 1843 on the site of the kitchen gardens of Kensington Palace, once housed a number of millionaires. It is now the home of many consulates and embassies but is still known as Millionaires' Row.

Millionaires' Square BRYANSTON SQUARE, near Marble Arch [2E 60b], built 1810-5 on an area known as Ward's

Field, was in the past known as Millionaires' Square, and some of the surrounding streets commemorate the Orchard-Portman family, the ground landlord from Bryanston in Dorset.

Milton, John (1608-74) Poet. Born in BREAD STREET, Cheapside [3D 61b], and educated at St Paul's School. He was blind for about the last twenty years of his life. His works include *L'Allegro*, *Il Penseroso*, *Lycidas*, *Paradise Lost* and *Paradise Regained*. He lived in PETTY FRANCE, St James's Park [2C 62c] and from 1662 until his death at 124 BUNHILL ROW, City [4C 46]. Buried in ST GILES CRIPPLEGATE, CITY.

Mincing Lane, Fenchurch Street [4A 61c] The centre of the tea and rubber trades. Originally called Mincheon Lane from the 'minchens' or nuns of the Priory of St Helen, Bishopsgate, who were the owners of the land.

Mint, Royal, Tower Hill [4B 61c] Built 1808-11 by Sir Robert Smirke and James Johnson. It is thought to occupy the site of Eastminster, a Cistercian Abbey. Up to 1808, when it came to its present quarters, the Mint was established in the TOWER OF LONDON (*see main entry*). The official head of the Mint is the Chancellor of the Exchequer. Previously all the coins of the realm and of many Commonwealth and foreign countries were struck here, but there is now a new Mint in South Wales where decimal coins are struck.

Mithras, Temple of In 1954 workmen excavating to build Bucklersbury House in Queen Victoria Street, City [3E 61a], unearthed the Roman Temple of Mithras—a Persian sun god whose cult was taken up by the Romans in the first century. The temple was reconstructed and put back near its original position after the building was completed. Sculpture from the temple is now in the GUILDHALL MUSEUM (*see Guildhall*).

Mobile Police The original Bow Street Police Court in COVENT GARDEN, opened in 1748, was the headquarters of the Robin Redbreasts, so-called because of their scarlet waistcoats. Better known as the Bow Street Runners, they were the first mobile police in this country. (*See also Police Station Lights.*)

Monument, Eastcheap [4F 61b] Built 1671-7 by Sir Christopher Wren to commemorate the fire of 1666. The column, said to be the tallest isolated stone column in the world, is 202 ft high and is exactly 202 ft from PUDDING LANE (*see main entry*), where the

The Monument.

fire started. In 1842, the gallery on top, from which there is a fine view, was railed off to prevent people committing suicide.

Moore, George (1852-1933) Novelist. His works include *Esther Waters, A Modern Lover* and the autobiographical *Confessions of a Young Man*. He lived from 1911 till his death at 121 EBURY STREET, Pimlico [4F 62b].

Moore, Thomas (1779-1852) Irish-born musician and poet, national lyrist of Ireland. His works include *Irish Melodies, Loves of the Angels* and *The Fudge Family in Paris*. He lived at 85 GEORGE STREET, Marble Arch [2E 60b]. Married in 1811 in ST MARTIN-IN-THE-FIELDS.

More, Sir Thomas (1478-1535) Statesman and author. Born in MILK STREET, Cheapside [4B 64] and educated at a school in THREADNEEDLE STREET. He entered Parliament at the age of twenty-one, was Chancellor of the Exchequer 1523-9, Speaker of the House of Commons 1520 and Lord High Chancellor 1529-32. His refusal to accept Henry VIII as head of the English Church led to his execution. There is a statue on the corner of SERLE STREET and CAREY STREET, Chancery Lane [3A 61a], and another in CHEYNE WALK, Chelsea [1A 76].

Mormon Chapel The Church of Jesus Christ of Latter Day Saints, Hyde Park Chapel in PRINCES GATE, Exhibition Road [2B 62a], was designed by Sir Thomas Bennet and opened in 1961. It was the first Mormon chapel to be built in London.

Morris, William (1834-96) Poet, artist and socialist, perhaps most famous as a decorator and craftsman. In 1862 he founded a firm to make furniture, wallpaper, etc. and in 1877 he founded the Society for the Protection of Ancient Buildings. His published works include *Sigurd the Volsung* and *The Earthly Paradise*. He lived 1856-9 at 17 RED LION SQUARE, Holborn [2F 60d], and from 1878 to the time of his death at KELMSCOTT HOUSE, Upper Mall, CHISWICK [4B 58]. There is a William Morris Gallery at WATER HOUSE, Forest Road, WALTHAMSTOW [3D 33] where he lived 1848-56.

Morse Code Samuel Morse (1791-1872), born in Massachusetts, USA, was a pioneer of electrical telegraphy and the inventor of morse code. The first morse code message was sent from Washington, DC, to Baltimore in 1844. In 1811 he lived at 92 GREAT TITCHFIELD STREET, Oxford Street [1B 60c], and 1812-5 at 143 CLEVELAND STREET [1B 60c], near where the GPO Tower now is.

Moscow Dumps During the early part of the nineteenth century, Kings Cross (*see main entry*) – or Battle Bridge as it was then called – was noted for its many dust heaps of cinders, filth and horse bones. These heaps were sold to the Russians as materials for the rebuilding of Moscow soon after Napoleon's disastrous campaign of 1812.

Motor Show The first exhibition was held in 1895 at Tunbridge Wells. The first Society of Motor Manufacturers and Traders Motor Show opened at the Crystal Palace, Sydenham in 1903, and two years later moved to the OLYMPIA, Hammersmith. From 1920 until 1922 the exhibition was held at both the White City and the Olympia which were linked by a coach service. From 1937 it has been held at the EARLS COURT STADIUM, Earls Court [4E 59].

Mount Street, Mayfair [4F 60b] Derives its name from Oliver's Mount, an inner ring of fortifications built by Cromwell's army in 1643 to defend London from the king's troops.

Mozart, Wolfgang Amadeus (1756-91) Born in Salzburg, he began to study music at the age of three and was a child prodigy. In 1762-79 he made a number of European tours, including visits to London. He wrote many symphonies, concertos, string quartets, and sonatas and several operas including *Don Giovanni* and *The Magic Flute*. In 1764, at the age of eight, he wrote his first symphony at 180 EBURY STREET, Pimlico, where he was then living [4F 62b].

Mulberry Gardens In 1609 James I tried to encourage the silk industry by importing a number of mulberry trees and planting them on the present site of BUCKINGHAM PALACE, then known as Mulberry Gardens. As the venture proved unprofitable, part of the estate was sold and was in due course bought by John Sheffield, who built Buckingham House (*see Buckingham Palace*).

Muscovy Street, Tower Hill [4A 61c] Derives its name from the first 'joint stock' company, the Muscovy Company. This association, which was founded in 1555 in order to trade with the Baltic countries, was important in helping to establish London as a great trading centre.

Music Halls London's first music hall, the Canterbury Hall in the Westminster Bridge Road, was opened in 1849 by a Mr Charles Morton and closed during the Second World War. The LONDON PALLADIUM, the home of variety, in ARGYLL STREET, Oxford Circus [3B 60c], was built on the site of Hengler's Circus and opened on 26 December 1910 with Nellie Wallace and Ella Sheilds as two of its main stars.

Musicians' Church Because the north chapel in the church of the HOLY SEPULCHRE, HOLBORN VIADUCT [2B 61a], is a musicians' memorial, the church is sometimes called the Musicians' Church. Until late in the eighteenth century the church presented condemned prisoners on their journey to Tyburn Gallows with a posy of flowers, and until 1890 they tolled the church bells for every execution. The church dates from the twelfth century, was rebuilt in the fifteenth century, repaired by Wren 1670-7 after the Great Fire and further restored in 1878 and 1950.

Muswell Hill [1D 29] Named after a well belonging to the Fraternity of St John of Jerusalem, Clerkenwell, who built a dairy here. The water from this spring was thought to cure scrofula, and so the Shrine of Our Lady in Muswell Hill became a pilgrimage centre.

N

Napier, Sir Charles James (1782-1853) British soldier and statesman. He fought in the Peninsular War and the American War, and distinguished himself in Sind which he governed until 1847. His statue in Trafalgar Square was erected by public subscription, but most of the contributions came from private soldiers with whom he was always popular.

Napier of Magdala, Robert Napier (1810-90) Field Marshal. He was present at the relief of Lucknow. In 1867 he commanded the Abyssinian expedition and was given a peerage for his brilliant storming of Magdala. He was appointed Constable of the Tower of London. Buried in St Paul's Cathedral. Statue on the north side of Queen's Gate, Kensington [2A 62a].

Napoleon III Louis Napoleon Bonaparte (1808-73), nephew of Napoleon I, was elected president of France in 1848 and proclaimed emperor in 1852. After his defeat by Bismarck in the Franco-Prussian War he found refuge in London. He lived 1846-8 at 1c King Street, St James's [1C 62c].

National Anthem The first known public performance of 'God Save the King' took place at Drury Lane Theatre, Covent Garden, on 28 September 1745. The score was prepared by Thomas Arne (*see main entry*), then leader of the orchestra at the theatre.

National Gallery [4D 60d] Founded in 1824 when the government purchased John Julius Angerstein's collection, first exhibited at his house at 100 Pall Mall. The present building in TRAFALGAR SQUARE, built 1834-8 on the site of the Royal Mews, was designed by William Wilkins. Its critics called it the National Cruet Stand, because they maintained that the cupolas looked like pepper-pots. In order to economize, the builder was compelled to use the old columns of the original CARLTON HOUSE (*see main entry*) which are incorporated into the portico. The gallery now houses one of the finest collections of paintings in the world, covering all periods and schools.

National Maritime Museum, Romsey Rd., Greenwich [1D 81] Centred on the QUEEN'S HOUSE which was built in 1618 by Inigo Jones for Anne of Denmark,

The Cutty Sark.

wife of James I, and completed in 1635 for Henrietta Maria, wife of Charles I. The Museum, opened in 1934, provides a survey of naval history from Tudor times to the present day and houses the greatest collection of sea pictures in the country, presented by Sir James Caird.

National Portrait Gallery, Trafalgar Square [4E 60d] Behind the National Gallery, in a building completed in 1896. The collection was founded in 1856 and contains over 4,500 portraits of 3,500 people, illustrating British history through the people themselves. Usually no picture is included until the subject has been dead ten years. The gallery contains works by many great artists, as well as representing figures of importance and interest.

Nelson, Lord Horatio (1758-1805) Admiral. He joined the Navy in 1770, lost his right eye in 1794 at the Battle of Calvi and three years later lost his right arm at the Battle of Santa Cruz. In 1798 he almost entirely destroyed the French fleet in the Battle of the Nile. He subsequently formed a liaison with Lady Emma Hamilton (*see main entry*). In 1805 he totally defeated the French and Spanish fleets at Trafalgar, but was killed in the battle. He lived at 103 and 147 NEW BOND STREET [3A 60c]. He was buried in ST PAUL'S CATHEDRAL in a coffin made of wood from *L'Orient*, a French flagship which he defeated. Monument in TRAFALGAR SQUARE.

Nelson's Column, Trafalgar Square [4E 60d] Erected between 1840 and 1843 from W. Railton's designs. The monument, 186 feet high, commemorates Nelson's victory over the combined French and Spanish forces. On the base are bronze reliefs, representing scenes from the battles of St Vincent, Nile, Copenhagen, and Trafalgar. The monument is annually decorated on Trafalgar Day, October 21st, the anniversary of the battle. The bronze lions were erected in 1867 from Sir Edwin Landseer's designs.

Nelson's Statue Mounted on the column in Trafalgar Square from E. H. Bailey's designs, is 17 feet 4½ inches high. The capital of the column was cast from the cannon of the British battleship 'The Royal George' that sank at Spithead in 1782 with the loss of its admiral and most of its crew.

New England Captain John Smith (1580-1631), soldier, went to America in 1606 with the founders of Virginia and two years later became their leader. Taken prisoner by the Indians, his life was spared thanks to the intercession of the twelve-year-old

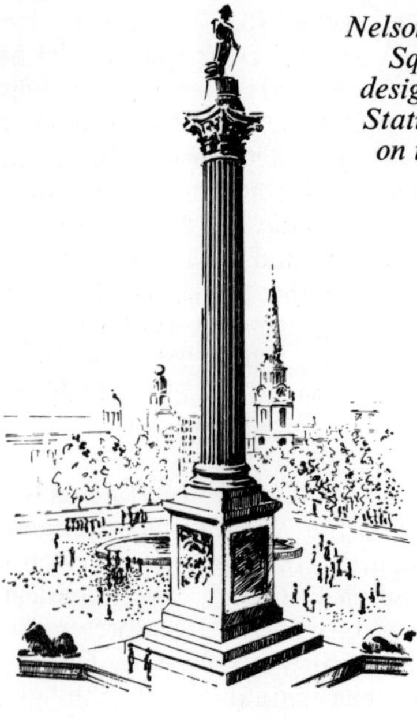

Nelson's Column, Trafalgar Square, erected from the designs of W. Railton. The Statue of Nelson, mounted on this column, was made from the designs of E. H. Baily.

Princess Pocahontas. He is credited with mapping out the coast of the area which he called New England. Buried in the church of the HOLY SEPULCHRE, HOLBORN VIADUCT [2C 61a]. Statue in BOW CHURCH PLACE, beside St Mary-le-Bow, Cheapside [3E 61b].

Newgate Prison Erected in the twelfth century on the site of the present OLD BAILEY (*see main entry*). Rebuilding of the prison began in 1770, but it was partially destroyed in 1780 by the Gordon Rioters who set a number of prisoners free, and work was not finished until 1782. In 1783 this prison replaced Tyburn as the main place of execution. The last public execution there was that of Michael Barrett, hanged on 26 May 1868 for attempting to blow up the Middlesex House of Detention. From then until 1901 executions took place inside the prison, and in 1902 the prison was demolished.

Newman, John Henry (1801-90) Cardinal. In 1824 he was ordained in the Church of England, but twenty-one years later he was received into the Roman Catholic Church and was created a cardinal in 1879. Elgar set to music his poem *The Dream of Gerontius*. His hymn 'Lead Kindly Light' is the best known of his works. He lived for a time when young at 17 SOUTHAMPTON PLACE, High Holborn [2F 60d]. Statue in forecourt at BROMPTON HOUSE adjoining Brompton Oratory, Brompton Road [3C 62a].

Newspapers The offices of the *Daily Courant*, England's first daily newspaper, opened in March 1702 on the south-west corner of LUDGATE HILL [3C 61a], and closed in 1735. The country's oldest surviving daily newspaper, *The Times*, was founded in 1785 in PRINTING HOUSE SQUARE (*see main entry*) by Mr John Walter (the brother of the founder of the Corps of Commissionaires—*see main entry*). It was at first called the *Daily Universal Register* but in 1788 the name was changed to *The Times*.

Newton, Sir Isaac (1642-1727) Natural philosopher, president of the Royal Society and master of the Mint. He was the English mathematician who first stated the laws of gravitation and light. Erected the first reflection telescope. He lived in ST MARTIN'S STREET, Leicester Square [4D 60d], (where the Westminster Reference Library now is) and at 87 JERMYN STREET, Piccadilly [4C 60c]. Buried in WESTMINSTER ABBEY.

New Zealand House, Haymarket [4D 60d] The headquarters of the High Commissioner for New Zealand, erected on the site of the Carlton Hotel. The London County Council, the Fine Arts Commissioner and the Crown Commissioners, who are the ground landlords, opposed the building's original design on the grounds it was too near the palace and the park, and too tall. However, it was opened on 9 May 1963 by Queen Elizabeth II, minus a few storeys.

Nicked Birds All swans on the Thames automatically belong to the Crown, with the exception of those belonging to the Dyers' and the Vintners' Companies. One Saturday in July the operation known as 'swan upping' is performed by the Swan Masters of these two companies, who set off in boats on the Thames to round up the cygnets. The Dyers make one nick on the beak of the birds, the Vintners two, but the royal birds are left untouched.

Nightingale, Florence (1820-1910) Hospital reformer who in 1854 went to the Crimea to modernize the military hospitals. She was loved by the British soldiers who called her the Lady with the Lamp. She founded the Florence Nightingale Hospital, LISSON GROVE, Marylebone [4B 44], and in 1908 received the

Freedom of the City of London. She lived in a house on the site of 5-10 SOUTH STREET, Park Lane [4F 60b]. Statue in WATERLOO PLACE, Pall Mall [4D 60d]. Memorial in ST PAUL'S CATHEDRAL.

No-Man's-Land A huge field known as Smoothfield (subsequently SMITHFIELD—*see main entry*) was a burial ground for victims of the 1349 Plague. It has been estimated that at least 60,000 people were buried here.

Norfolk House, St James's Square [4C 60c] The third on its site. The original house was the home of Frederick, Prince of Wales 1737-41, and here his son, George III was born in 1738. The second, which stood 1748-1935, was built for the ninth Duke of Norfolk. The present one, a handsome block of offices, was from 24 June till 8 November 1942 the Allied Headquarters under the Supreme Command of General Dwight Eisenhower.

North-West Passage Sir John Franklin (1786-1847), Arctic explorer, in 1845 set out from the Royal Dockyard, Woolwich, in search of the north-west passage. His fate was unknown until 1859 when records were discovered showing that he had actually discovered the north-west passage, but that the entire expedition, including Franklin, had perished. Statue in WATERLOO PLACE, Pall Mall [4D 60d].

Norwood Presumed to have been a wood that lay north of Croydon. GIPSY ROAD and GIPSY HILL, West Norwood [4C 94], are said to mark the area where the gipsies set up their headquarters when they first came to England.

O

Old-Age Pensions Henry Herbert Asquith (1852-1928), Liberal statesman and lawyer, entered Parliament in 1886, was home secretary 1892-5 and, as chancellor of exchequer, in 1906 introduced the Old-Age Pensions Bill. He was prime minister 1908-16 and in 1925 was created a peer. He lived at 20 Cavendish Square, Oxford Circus [2A 60C], and 44 Bedford Square, Bloomsbury [2D 60d].

Old Bailey [3C 61a] The usual name for the Central Criminal Court, which stands at the junction of Newgate Street and Old Bailey and is the chief criminal court for Greater London. Occupying the site of Newgate Prison, it was built in 1902-7 by E. W. Mountford. The main hall was damaged by bombs in 1941 but has since been restored. The bronze figure of Justice that surmounts the copper dome is the work of F. W. Pomeroy.

Oldest Hospital Bart's, or St Bartholomew's Hospital, Smithfield [2C 61a], London's oldest hospital, was founded in 1123 on its present site by Rahere (d.1144), king's jester to Henry I. During a pilgrimage to Rome, Rahere was taken ill with fever and made a vow that if he recovered he would build an establishment for the sick in honour of St Bartholomew. The hospital was refounded by Henry VIII in 1546 and the gatehouse erected in 1702.

Oldest Restaurant Rule's 35 Maiden Lane, Covent

The Old Bailey, London's Central Criminal Court.

Garden [4E 60d], was established by the Rule family in 1798, mainly as an oyster bar. It still stands on its original site and is the oldest surviving restaurant in London.

Old Jewry, Bank [3E 61b] The quarter occupied by the Jews before they were expelled by Edward I in 1290.

Old Roman Road Roman Road and Old Ford Road, Bethnal Green [4F 47], were used by the Romans to get to the old ford.

One-Man Police Station On the south-east side of TRAFALGAR SQUARE there is a hollow pillar with a lamp on top which houses one policeman who has telephone communication with Cannon Street Police Station. This forerunner of the present-day police box is the smallest police station in London.

Oriental Avenue Gerrard Street, Shaftesbury Avenue [3D 60d], was built about 1677 and named after Lord Gerrard, Earl of Macclesfield, whose residence, Macclesfield House, stood nearby. As this street contains many Chinese and Indian restaurants, it is often called Oriental Avenue or Eastern Avenue.

P

Padded Cell Because of the furnishings of its trains, the world's first electric tube, running from King William Street to Stockwell, became known as the 'padded cell'. The line was opened on 4 November 1890 by King Edward VII, then Prince of Wales.

Palace of Savoy Built in 1247 on the site of the present Savoy Hotel [4F 60d] by Henry III (1216-72), for Peter, Count of Savoy, his wife's uncle. Subsequently the palace passed to John of Gaunt, Duke of Lancaster, and in 1381 Wat Tyler's rebels destroyed it on their march to London. Rebuilt, it was converted into a hospital by Henry VII in 1550 and was used as such until 1702. The Savoy Hotel was built in 1889. (*See also Queen's Chapel of the Savoy.*)

Pall Mall [4D 60d] Built about 1661 on a field where '*paille-maille*', an old French game resembling croquet, was played. The game, pronounced 'pell-mell', gave its name to this street and also to the Mall, the approach to Buckingham Palace.

Palmerston, Henry (1784-1865) Whig statesman. Born at 20 Queen Anne's Gate, St James's Park [2D 62d]. He entered Parliament in 1807 and was prime minister 1855-8 and 1859-65. He was popular with the people, but tended to annoy the Queen and other ministers. He lived at 4 Carlton Gardens, Pall Mall [1D 62d], and from 1855 until his death at 94 Piccadilly [4B 60c]. Buried in Westminster Abbey. Statue in Parliament Square.

Pankhurst, Emmeline (1858-1928) Suffragette. In 1889 she helped to found the Women's Franchise League and was imprisoned three times for her activities. In 1903 she founded the Women's Social and Political Union headquarters at 3 CLEMENT'S INN, Strand [3A 61a], and encouraged the militant campaign. Monument in the VICTORIA TOWER GARDENS [2E 62d].

Panton Street, Haymarket [4D 60d] Named after a Colonel Thomas Panton, owner of a gaming-house in Piccadilly. In one night, he won a fortune at cards and dice and swore he would never gamble again. He invested the money he won in real estate. (*See also Film Industry.*)

Parish Churches ST MARTIN-IN-THE-FIELDS (*see main entry*), Trafalgar Square, being within the precincts of Buckingham Palace, is known as the royal parish church. ST LAWRENCE JEWRY (*see City Church*), Gresham Street, is the official church of the City Corporation of London. ST MARGARET'S, Westminster (*see Parliament's Church*), has been the parish church for the House of Commons since 1614. ST BARTHOLOMEW THE GREAT, Smithfield, founded by Rahere, the court jester (*see also Hospital*), is the oldest parish church in Greater London. ST MARY ABBOTS, Church Street, Kensington [3F 59], built by Sir Gilbert Scott in 1869-72, has the tallest parish-church spire in London. It is 278 ft high.

Parliament Hill, Hampstead [1B 44] Thought to be so named from the Parliamentary generals who placed cannons here for the defence of London during the Civil War.

Parliament's Church ST MARGARET'S church, adjoining Westminster Abbey [2E 62d] was built in about 1190 as the parish church of Westminster, rebuilt in

1504-23 and restored in 1878. Pepys, Milton and Sir Winston Churchill (*see main entries*) were all married here. Since 1614 it has been the parish church for the use of the House of Commons.

Parson's Green [2E 75] A triangular green situated on the north side of New King's Road, Fulham. It is so called from the parsonage house of the parish of Fulham, demolished in about the year 1740.

Paternoster Row, St Paul's Cathedral [3D 61b] So called either because of the makers of rosaries, or paternosters, who worked here or because pre-Reformation Catholic processions began their paternoster – the Lord's prayer – at this point. (*See Amen Corner*).

Patmore, Coventry (1823-96) Poet. Born in Woodford. For twenty years assistant librarian at the British Museum, his works include *The Angel in the House* and *The Unknown Eros.* He was married at ST JOHN'S HAMPSTEAD [1A 44], and lived 1863-4 at 14 PERCY STREET, Tottenham Court Road [2D 60d].

Pauper's Paradise Hammersmith Infirmary, now HAMMERSMITH HOSPITAL, Du'Cane Road, WHITE CITY [2a 58], was built in 1905. Because it gave its poor patients the most up-to-date treatment, it earned the name of the Pauper's Paradise. In this hospital Siamese twins were first separated and one of the world's first kidney transplants took place.

Pawnbroker's Tavern The Castle, in COWCROSS STREET, Farringdon Road [1C 61a], is the only tavern to have a pawnbroker's licence. George IV, gambling one night in the neighbourhood, lost his money and the owners of the inn lent him some, on the security of his watch. This was redeemed and later the pawnbroker's licence was sent.

Peach Melba Auguste Escoffier (1845-1935), originally chef on the staff of Napoleon III, came to London to be chef at the Carlton Hotel, Haymarket, and then at the Savoy Hotel, Strand. In 1892, at the Savoy, he invented Peach Melba in honour of Dame Nellie Melba, the singer.

Peckham Hill Street, Peckham [2E 79] Occupies the garden site of the manor house said to have been built in 1672 by Sir Thomas Bond, the builder of BOND STREET (*see main entry*), and acquired by a Mrs Hill in about 1731.

Pedlar's Acre There is a tradition that early in the sixteenth century a pedlar gave a piece of land worth 2s 8d to St Mary's Church, Lambeth, on condition that there should always be a window bearing a picture of his dog and himself in the church. His wish was complied with and the window was even replaced after being destroyed in the Blitz in 1941. The land, which was known as Pedlar's Acre, was bought by the London County Council in 1910 at a cost of £81,000 in order to build COUNTY HALL (*see main entry*). The part of Pedlar's Acre which is now BELVEDERE ROAD [1F 62d] used to be called Church Osier in the sixteenth century because there was a huge osier bed there. Osier; a species of willow used in basket-work.

Peel, Sir Robert (1788-1850) Conservative statesman. Educated at Harrow School. Home secretary 1822-7 and 1828-30, prime minister 1834-5 and 1841-6. He founded the Metropolitan Police Force and introduced Catholic emancipation, but fell from power because of his Repeal of the Corn Laws. In Constitution Hill, Green Park, he was thrown from his horse and died from his injuries. Statues in PARLIAMENT SQUARE, POSTMEN'S PARK, Aldersgate Street (*see main entry*) and WESTMINSTER ABBEY.

Penicillin Sir Alexander Fleming (1881-1955) in 1929 discovered penicillin on a second-floor laboratory in St Mary's Hospital, Praed Street, Paddington. He was knighted in 1944 and a year later shared the Nobel Prize for medicine with Sir Howard Florey. Fleming died at 20a DANVERS STREET, Cheyne Walk [1B 76]. His ashes are in the crypt of ST PAUL'S CATHEDRAL.

Penny Newspaper The *Daily Telegraph*, one of the leading national newspapers, was first published by a Colonel Sleigh in June 1855, in FLEET STREET and consisted of a single sheet costing twopence. The colonel, failing to make it a success, sold it. His enterprising successor reduced the price to one penny making it the first penny daily newspaper.

Penny Post Sir Rowland Hill (1795-1879) introduced the penny post in 1840. As secretary to the Post Office 1834-64, he invented the adhesive stamp. He lived at 1 ORME SQUARE, Bayswater Road [2F 59]. Buried in WESTMINSTER ABBEY. Statue outside the GPO, KING EDWARD STREET, City [2D 61b].

Pennsylvania, USA William Penn (1644-1718), born in the City of London, baptized at ALL HALLOWS BY THE TOWER, Eastcheap [3F 61b], served a prison sentence for his Quaker beliefs. With his own money he purchased land for a Quaker colony in the New World, founding Pennsylvania (named after him), one of the thirteen original American states.

Pensioner's Record On 12 October 1935, when Chelsea Football Club, known as 'The Pensioners', played Arsenal on their home ground (Stamford Bridge, Fulham), there were 82,905 spectators in attendance, a record gate for an English football league game.

Pentonville Road, King's Cross [4F 45] Built on the site of a priory that belonged to the Knights Hospitallers of St John's, Clerkenwell. The road commemorates the name of the owner and builder of the estate, Mr Henry Penton (*d.*1812), Member of Parliament and Lord of the Admiralty.

Pepys, Samuel (1633-1703) Diarist. Baptized at St Bride's Fleet Street, educated at St Paul's School. He was secretary to the Admiralty (1673-88), held several public appointments and worked as a clerk under Sir George Downing (*see Downing Street*) when the latter was secretary to the Treasury. He married in 1655 at St Margaret's, Westminster, (*see Parliament's Church*). His diary, written in his own version of shorthand and undeciphered until 1825, gives a complete and intimate picture of the life of his time. He lived 1679-88 at 12 BUCKINGHAM STREET, Adelphi [4E 60d] and next door at No. 14 from 1688-1701. He died at a house on the site of 29 NORTH SIDE, CLAPHAM COMMON [4c 76], and is buried in ST OLAVES (*see main entry*), Hart Street, Tower Hill.

Peter Pan Statue Erected in 1912 in KENSINGTON GARDENS at the expense of Sir James Barrie (1860-1937), the author of *Peter Pan.* The story is that Sir James had the statue put up at night, so that the children would think the fairies put it there. His works also include the plays *The Admirable Crichton* and *Mary Rose.* He lived at 100 BAYSWATER ROAD [3C 60a], and, 1911-37, at 2 ROBERT STREET, Strand [4E 60d].

Peter the Great (1672-1725) In 1682 he became czar of Russia. He founded St Petersburg and modernized Russia on western lines. He came to London in 1698 to learn carpentry and shipbuilding, and lived at Sayes Court, Deptford, the residence of John Evelyn, the diarist (*see Evelyn Street*), and later at 15 BUCKING-

HAM STREET, Adelphi [4E 60d] CZAR STREET, Deptford [1B 80], is named after him.

Physic Gardens In 1620 John Tradescant (*d.*1637), naturalist and gardener to Charles I, introduced to this country the Algier apricot. In his home in South Lambeth, by Vauxhall Cross, he established England's first physic garden. Buried in ST MARY'S Church, LAMBETH [3A 63a]. TRADESCANT ROAD, South Lambeth Road [2F 77], commemorates both his and his son's name.

Piccadilly Circus [4C 60c] Famous for its neon advertisements at night. The circular underground station, opened in 1928, is the largest in London. The name Piccadilly comes from 'pickadille'—a kind of high collar popular in the eighteenth century. A tailor

Peter Pan. Erected in Kensington Gardens at the expense of Sir James Barrie, the author of Peter Pan.

who made this type of neckwear built himself a house (since demolished) in what is now GREAT WINDMILL STREET; it was popularly called Pickadille Hall and the name spread to the whole area.

Pill Island Harley Street and Wimpole Street [2A 60c], inhabited mainly by medical specialists, were called Pill Island by the old hansom-cab drivers.

Pillory On 24 June 1830, a Mr Bossy was put in the pillory for one hour at the Old Bailey for committing perjury. This was the last occasion on which the pillory was used.

Pitt, William (1707-78), First Earl of Chatham, known as Pitt the Elder He entered Parliament in 1735 as a Whig and became prime minister in 1756, but because of ill health resigned in 1768. Under his administration, Clive (*see main entry*) won the Battle of Plassey and the French fleet was defeated at Quiberon Bay. He lived at CHATHAM HOUSE (*see main entry*), St James's Square. Buried in WESTMINSTER ABBEY. Statue in the GUILDHALL.

Pitt, William (1759-1806), known as Pitt the Younger Son of Pitt the Elder, he entered Parliament as a Tory in 1781. He was prime minister 1783-1801, the youngest man ever to hold this office, and again from 1804 until his death. He was responsible for re-organizing the national finances and the Act of Union with Ireland. He tried to build up a coalition with Austria and Russia against Napoleon and died broken-hearted after the defeat of Austerlitz. He lived 1803-4 at 120 BAKER STREET [1E 60b]. Buried in WESTMINSTER ABBEY. Statue in HANOVER SQUARE, Regent Street [3B 60c].

Plimsoll Line Samuel Plimsoll (1824-98), Member of

Parliament for Derby 1868-80, agitated for safety at sea. His attacks on the shipping owners brought about the Merchant Shipping Act of 1876 which compelled every cargo ship to be marked with a white line, now known as the Plimsoll Line, indicating the safety load line. His statue in Embankment Gardens, VICTORIA EMBANKMENT [4F 60d], is inscribed 'To the sailors' friend'.

Police Station Lights BOW STREET is the only police station in central London to have white lamps instead of the traditional blue. The lamps were paid for by Queen Victoria; some claim that she wished to see the opera house better at night, but others maintain that she wanted to disguise the fact that there was a police station opposite her beloved opera house.

Police Strike The Metropolitan and City Police were infuriated when they were refused permission to join the newly founded Police Union and denied an increase in their weekly wage, so on 29 August 1918, at midnight, they came out on strike. Two days later, through the efforts of Lloyd George, the prime minister, the strike finished with the police accepting a 13s pay rise.

Poor Carlton The Carlton Club, founded in 1832 by the Duke of Wellington, the premier Conservative Club transferred to its present quarters at No. 69, St. James's Street, SW1, when its original home in Pall Mall was bombed in 1940.

Pope, Alexander (1688-1744) Poet. Born in PLOUGH COURT, Lombard Street [3F 61b]. He quickly made a reputation for himself with his satirical poetry and translations of Homer, his most famous works being *Essay on Criticism*, *The Rape of Lock* and *Essay on Man*. In 1719 he settled in Twickenham and is buried in the parish church of ST MARY, Church Street, TWICKENHAM [2F 87].

Poplar Mayor Poplar, in the borough of Tower Hamlets, was originally a hamlet of Stepney and derives its name from the mass of poplar trees that grew there. William Crooks, who went to a workhouse school, was in 1901 the Mayor of Poplar, and had the honour of being London's first Labour mayor. Crooks was elected to Parliament and later became a Privy Councillor. Buried in TOWER HAMLETS CEMETERY, Southern Grove, Mile End [4B 48].

Porridge Island Before TRAFALGAR SQUARE was built in 1829 the area, which contained numerous slums, very narrow streets and many cook shops, was known as Porridge Island.

Porter's Rest This resting place was erected in 1861 by the Vestry of St George's, Hanover Square, on the pavement of PICCADILLY, near the railings of Green Park, to enable porters carrying produce to and from Covent Garden on their backs to place their loads on it while they had a short rest.

Portland Stone BANQUETING HOUSE, Whitehall [1E 62d], the main surviving part of the royal Palace of Whitehall—entrance in Horse Guards Avenue. Built by Inigo Jones in 1619-22, was possibly the first major London building to be built in Portland stone.

Postal Districts Until the formation of Greater London in 1965, London had 118 sub-postal districts, Fenchurch Street being the smallest and Chingford the largest. Numbering of postal districts was introduced in 1917 to assist the unskilled postal sorters employed during the First World War.

Postmen's Park The gardens attached to the Church of St Botolph in Aldersgate Street [1D 61b], adjacent to the General Post Office Buildings, are known as the Postmen's Park. In these gardens G. F. Watts (1817-1904), artist, erected an arcade containing memorials to a number of civilians who died saving other people's lives.

Post Office The post office in ST MARTIN'S PLACE, Trafalgar Square [4E 60d], is open twenty-four hours a day, 365 days in the year, and has the largest post-office counter in Europe.

Post Office Prisons Mount Pleasant Parcel Office, ROSEBERY AVENUE [1A 61a], was built in 1900 on the site of Coldbath Fields House of Correction, a prison from 1794 to 1877. The rear exit of the GPO in GILTSPUR STREET [2C 61a], adjacent to Bart's Hospital, stands on the site of the Giltspur Compter, a debtors' prison from 1791 to 1855.

Post Office Railway Runs underground from Whitechapel to Paddington via Liverpool Street Station, the GPO building in the City and Mount Pleasant. It is 6½ miles long and opened in 1928. The trains, electrically driven and automatically controlled, travel at a speed of 35 mph.

Premier Conservative Club The Carlton Club, founded in 1832 by the Duke of Wellington, transferred to its present quarters at 69 St James's Street, Piccadilly [4B 60c], when its original home in Pall Mall was bombed in 1941.

Primrose Hill [2B 44] On the north side of Regent's Park, was so named from the masses of primroses that once grew there. The Primrose League was formed in 1883 in memory of Benjamin Disraeli whose favourite flower was the primrose. Primrose Day is celebrated on April 9th, the anniversary of Disraeli's death.

Prince Henry's Room 17 FLEET STREET [3B 61a], built about 1611, the oldest building in Fleet Street, is thought to have contained the chamber in which Prince Henry (*d.* 1612), the elder son of James I, held his council meetings. The room still has the seventeenth-century ceiling and panelling.

Princess Sculptress The white marble statue of Queen Victoria that stands in front of KENSINGTON PALACE (*see London Museum*) is the work of her daughter, Princess Louise, who died in the palace in 1939.

Printing House Square [3C 61a] So called because the King's Printing House was established here in the seventeenth century. In 1665 at the King's Printing House the *London Gazette*, the official government newspaper, published three times a week and the oldest newspaper in the country, was first published. In this square in 1814 England's first steam printing press was installed. (*See also Newspapers.*)

Prison The Fleet Prison, which occupied the site of 14 FARRINGDON STREET, Ludgate Circus [2C 61a], was known to be in existence in the twelfth century and was converted into a debtors' prison in 1641. Destroyed by the fire of 1666 and again during the Gordon Riots of 1780, it was twice rebuilt but finally demolished in 1846. It was in the Congregational Memorial Hall built on its site in 1874 (demolished 1971) that the Labour Party was founded. From here the Trades Union Council directed the General Strike in 1926.

Prisoner-Bishop Ranulf Flambard, Bishop of Durham, who is credited with completing the White

Tower in the TOWER OF LONDON (*see main entry*) for Henry I, became in 1101 the first of the Tower's many prisoners and, in the same year, the first to escape.

Prisoners' Prison WORMWOOD SCRUBS PRISON, Du Cane Road, White City [2A 58], was built in 1874 by the convicts, from designs by Sir Edmund Du Cane, the penal reformer.

Pub Crawl In 1824 the workers erecting ST LUKE'S, Sydney Street, CHELSEA [4C 62a] (the church where Charles Dickens was married in 1836), built an underground tunnel that led to The Builders' Arms, a tavern in Britten Street.

Public Services In 1542 a Bill was passed to authorize the paving of certain streets; DUKE OF YORK STREET, St James's was the first to be paved in London. In 1854 the first pillar box was erected in FLEET STREET. In 1879 the first telephone exchange opened with ten subscribers in LOMBARD STREET.

Pudding Lane, Eastcheap [4F 61b] In this street in 1666 a greedy boy who stole a cake from a baker's shop accidentally started the Great Fire of London which lasted three days, causing the destruction of 13,000 houses and 400 streets and the loss of eleven lives.

Punch The magazine *Punch* was first published in July 1841, with its office at 85 FLEET STREET. One of its founders and its first editor was Henry Mayhew (1812-87), author of *London Labour and the London Poor*, who lived at 55 ALBANY STREET, Regent's Park [4D 45]

Punch and Judy This children's puppet drama, which originated in Italy, was introduced to London in 1662 and first staged under the portico of ST PAUL'S, COVENT GARDEN (*see Actors' Church*).

Q

Queen's Chapel of the Savoy, Savoy Street, Strand [4F 60d] Although the Palace of the Savoy (*see main entry*) is now gone the chapel, originally built in 1505, was rebuilt in the same style after a fire in 1864. It is the private property of the monarch (whether male or female) as Duke of Lancaster. The chapel contains a memorial window to Queen Mary and George V.

Queen's Elm Elizabeth I allegedly sheltered from a thunderstorm under a tree which grew on the site of the pub called The Queen's Elm at 241 Fulham Road [4B 62a].

R

Rag, The Army and Navy Club, St James's Square [4C 60c], founded in 1837 and rebuilt in 1963. It is called 'The Rag' because in about 1860 a Captain Duff, a member of the club, not liking the lunch served to him, rose from the table and shouted 'Is this the Rag and Famished Club?'

Raglan, Lord (1788-1855) He served under the Duke of Wellington during the Peninsular War and lost an arm at the Battle of Waterloo. He commanded the British forces in the Crimea, and was blamed unjustly for the losses incurred. The raglan sleeve is named after him. He lived at 5 Stanhope Gate, Park Lane [4F 60b].

Rail Fatality William Huskisson (1770-1830), Member of Parliament, in 1826 introduced the Bill that resulted in the construction of the Manchester-Liverpool line. Ironically, on 15 September 1830, when he was opening the line, he was killed by Stephenson's *Rocket*, thereby becoming the first rail fatality. He lived at 28 St James's Place, St James's Street [4B 60c]. Statue in Pimlico Gardens, Grosvenor Road [1D 77].

Rainfall In June 1903 58½ hours of continuous rain fell in Camden Square, Camden Road, the longest rainfall ever recorded in this country to date.

Raleigh, Sir Walter (c. 1552-1618) He served at sea against the Spaniards and was knighted by Elizabeth I. After James I's accession he was condemned to death for treason, but was instead imprisoned in the TOWER OF LONDON, where he wrote his *History of the World*. Released in 1616, he went on an unsuccessful expedition in search of gold and on his return was sentenced to death on the old charge and beheaded in Old Palace Yard. Buried in ST MARGARET'S, WESTMINSTER. Statue in WHITEHALL.

Rat's Hole The small tunnel that led from York Road to the cab rank attached to Platform 11 at Waterloo Station (before Leake Street was built) was called the Rats' Hole by the London cabbies. Abolished as a cab rank in 1963, it is still used by the vans of the General Post Office.

Ravensbourne, Deptford Legend has it that when Caesar and his thirsty army went looking for water they followed a raven which led them to a well. From then on it was called the raven's well, hence Ravensbourne (a bourne is a stream or brook).

Red Cross The international agency began in 1864. The British Red Cross Society, founded in 1870, was granted a Royal Charter in 1908. The Society, which originally aimed to assist prisoners and the wounded in war, today concerns itself with disasters which take place in peace time too. The national headquarters are at 8 GROSVENOR CRESCENT, Hyde Park Corner [2F 62b].

Red Lion Square, Holborn [2F 60d] Laid out in 1684 by Nicholas Barbon (1640-98), a famous speculative builder, on the site of Red Lion Fields.

Reform Chef The REFORM CLUB, the leading Liberal club at 104 PALL MALL [1C 62c], was founded in 1832 and built to Sir Charles Barry's designs. During the Crimean War (1854-56), Alex Soyer, the club's Chef, went to the front at his own expense to improve the cooking for the armed forces. At the same time, he invented some new cooking stoves.

Regent's Canal Starting at Paddington, where it connects with the Grand Junction Canal, the canal passes through 'Little Venice', as the area round BLOMFIELD ROAD [1A 60a] is called, and at long last joins the Thames at Limehouse. The canal was begun in 1812 and opened in 1820. It still carries a certain amount of traffic and during the summer there are boat trips starting from Little Venice and The Zoological Gardens.

Regent's Park [4C 44] Occupies the site of Marylebone Park, a former royal hunting-ground. It was laid out in 1812 by John Nash for the Prince Regent (later George IV), after whom it was named and who planned to buy one of the villas which were to be built here. Nash also built the Regency terraces which enclose the southern portion of the park. The park was opened to the public in 1838, and contains a lake, a pond, gardens, playing fields, an open-air theatre and the Zoo (*see main entry*).

Regents Canal.

Regular Street Great Queen Street, Kingsway [2F 60d], was known as the first regular street, because the houses, built by William Newton (*d.*1643), followed a uniform pattern. The street is named after Queen Henrietta Maria, wife of Charles I. NEWTON STREET, off Great Queen Street, commemorates the builder, who was claimed by many to be the first great speculator in land property.

Repeal/Re–peel On the Whitefriars Street side of 67 FLEET STREET [3B 61a] is a memorial tablet, stating that on this site in the years 1844-6 stood the London offices of the Anti Corn Law League with which John Bright and Richard Cobden (*see main entry*) were so closely associated. Attached to the front of the same building is a memorial tablet to Thomas Tompion (1638-1713), known as the father of English clock-making, and George Graham (1673-1751), clock-maker, who lived in a house on this site and are both buried in WESTMINSTER ABBEY.

Reuter's The international news agency was founded in 1851 by Paul Julius Reuter in a small office in Royal Exchange Buildings, Bank, and moved to 80 FLEET STREET [3B 61a], its present quarters, in 1939. Its founder originally used carrier pigeons to be the first with the news, but later had his own cables built when he found that public ones were too slow.

Reynolds, Sir Joshua (1723-93) Painter. In 1768 he was elected the first president of the Royal Academy of Arts (*see main entry*). The following year he was knighted, and in 1784 received the appointment of painter-in-ordinary to George III. He is famous for his portraits. From 1753-61 he lived at 5 GREAT NEWPORT STREET, Charing Cross Road [3E 60d]. Buried in ST PAUL'S CATHEDRAL. Monument in the forecourt of the ROYAL ACADEMY, Piccadilly.

Richard I (1157-99) Son of Henry II, called the Lion Heart, he came to the throne in 1189 and a year later set sail on his Crusades. After his two attempts to capture Jerusalem had failed, he was taken prisoner in 1192 by the Duke of Austria and ransomed, the money being paid by his subjects. Richard waged war against France and was killed at Chlâus. Statue in OLD PALACE YARD, near the House of Lords.

Roberts, Frederick Sleigh, first earl (1832-1914) Field marshal. He won the Victoria Cross in 1858 for service during the Indian Mutiny, fought in the Abyssinian campaign and, in the Afghan War, made a historical march to relieve the British forces at Kandahar, where he won a great victory. He was commander-in-chief of India (1885-93) and Ireland (1895-9), and commanded the British troops in South Africa during the Boer War. He retired from the army in 1904 but died visiting the trenches during the First World War. He lived at 47 PORTLAND PLACE, Oxford Circus [1A 60c]. Buried in ST PAUL'S CATHEDRAL. Statue in HORSEGUARDS PARADE, St James's Park [1D 62d].

Romilly, Sir Samuel (1757-1818) One of England's greatest law reformers. Born in FRITH STREET, Soho [3D 60d], Member of Parliament for Westminster and solicitor general in 1806, he introduced a number of laws abolishing the death sentence for various minor offences. He lived 1778-91 at 6 GRAY'S INN SQUARE, Holborn [1A 61a]. Soon after the death of his wife, he cut his throat and died instantly at his residence at 23 RUSSELL SQUARE, Holborn [1E 60d].

Romney, George (1734-1802) Cabinet-maker who became a self-taught artist and one of the most successful portrait painters of his day. He came to London in 1762. His paintings include portraits of Lady Hamilton (*see main entry*), Mr and Mrs Lindon and Jacob Morland. He lived 1797-9 at Romney House, 4 HOLLY BUSH HILL, Hampstead [1A 44].

Roosevelt, Franklin Delano (1882-1945) Thirty-second American president (Democrat), the only president of the USA to be elected four times consecutively. Stricken by infantile paralysis in 1921, he suffered its effects all his life. With Churchill he drew up the Atlantic Charter and attended the wartime conferences. On the base of his statue in GROSVENOR SQUARE, Mayfair (*see main entry*), are inscribed the words, 'Freedom of speech, freedom from want, freedom from fear and freedom to worship'.

Roosevelt, Theodore (1858-1919) Twenty-sixth American president (Republican) and the original 'Teddy Bear'. Governor of New York State and twice president of the USA. On 3 December 1886 he married Edith Carow at ST GEORGE'S, HANOVER SQUARE [3B 60c].

Rosebery Avenue Called after Archibald Philip Primrose, fifth earl of Rosebery (1847-1929). Born at 20 CHARLES STREET, Mayfair [4A 60c], in 1888 he was elected first chairman of the London County Council and six years later he succeeded Gladstone as prime minister.

Rosetta Stone A slab of basalt with a trilingual inscription which was found near Rosetta in the Nile delta in 1799 and is now preserved in the BRITISH MUSEUM (*see main entry*). It provided the key to the interpretation of Egyptian hieroglyphics. Thomas Young (1773-1829), an English scientist who was one of the first to decipher the Rosetta Stone, lived at 48 WELBECK STREET, Wigmore Street [2A 60c].

Rossetti, Dante Gabriel (1828-82) Painter and poet,

member of the Pre-Raphaelite group of artists. Born on the site of Rossetti House, HALLAM STREET, Portland Place [1B 60c]. His best-known paintings are 'Beata Beatrix' and 'Dante's Dream'. He lived at 17 RED LION SQUARE, Holborn [2F 60d], and 16 CHEYNE WALK, Chelsea [1A 76], where he had a menagerie in the garden. Buried in HIGHGATE CEMETERY.

Rosslyn Hill, Hampstead [1B 44] Derives its name from Rosslyn House, of which the grounds extended over most of the area now covered by ROSSLYN HILL, THURLOW ROAD and WEDDERBURN ROAD. Rosslyn House was the residence of Alexander Wedderburn, first Earl of Rosslyn (1733-1805), Member of Parliament, solicitor general and in 1793 lord chancellor. As a politician he was disliked because he allegedly flirted with both the Tories and the Whigs.

Rotherhithe Tunnel [3A 64] The original Rotherhithe and Wapping Tunnel, designed by Sir Marc Isambard Brunel (*see Brunel, Father and Son*), closed in 1866. The present vehicular tunnel which also runs from Wapping to Rotherhithe was built 1904-8 for the London County Council.

Rothschild Family Famous for their international banking and financial activities. Nathan Mayer Rothschild (1776-1836) came to England from Germany in 1797. During the Napoleonic Wars he gave financial assistance to the nation and, through the pigeon post which he set up, was the first to announce the victory of Waterloo. Nathan Mayer is buried in a now disused cemetery in BRADY STREET, Whitechapel Road [1D 61d]. His grandson Nathaniel (1840-1915) was created a baron in 1885.

Roundabout In 1926 Parliament Square became the birthplace in Britain of the traffic roundabout system.

Round Buildings Chelsea House, at 24 LOWNDES STREET, Knightsbridge [2E 62b], which is ten storeys high with a semi-circular façade, is called by the residents the Round House. To cab drivers, however, it is known as the Gasometer.

The TEMPLE CHURCH, FLEET STREET [3B 61a], consists of two parts, a nave and a chapel, known as the 'Round' and the 'Oblong' respectively.

Royal Academy of Arts [4B 60c] BURLINGTON HOUSE, Piccadilly, the home of the Royal Academy, was built in about 1715 by Richard Boyle, third earl of Burlington and Cork, with further additions in 1866-9 and 1874. The Academy was founded in 1768 in Pall Mall. In 1780 it moved to Somerset House and then in 1837 to the National Gallery, where it remained until 1869 when it came to Burlington House. The Royal Academy Summer Exhibition shows works by living British artists and there are other exhibitions during the rest of the year.

Royal Academy of Music [1F 60b] Founded in 1822 by the eleventh earl of Westmorland to promote music. In 1830 George IV granted the Academy a Royal Charter, and his successors, from William IV to the present sovereign, Queen Elizabeth, have all been royal patrons. The present building in MARYLEBONE ROAD was erected in 1910 and designed by Sir Ernest George and Alfred B. Yeates.

Royal CUP FINAL It was at the CRYSTAL PALACE, Sydenham, that royalty attended a FA cup final for the first time. On 25 April 1914 George V saw Burnley beat Everton 1-0. After the game he presented the cup and the medals.

Royal Matinée The first royal matinée film première was held on 22 December 1970 at the ABC theatre,

Shaftesbury Avenue. In attendance were Princess Margaret, Princess Alexandra and several of the royal children. The film, *The Railway Children*, was shown on behalf of two charities, the Invalid Children's Aid Association and the Children's Country Holiday Fund.

Royal Naval College, Greenwich [1D 81] Moved here from Lewisham. The college, for the education of naval officers, occupies a group of buildings erected 1696-9 by Sir Christopher Wren as Greenwich Hospital on the site of the palace where Henry VIII and his two daughters were born (*see Greenwich*). The hospital was originally a home for aged and disabled sailors until 1869, when the inmates were given pensions instead. Here Lord Nelson (*see main entry*) lay in state before being taken to St Paul's Cathedral for burial. The fine PAINTED HALL and CHAPEL of the Hospital are open to the public.

Royal Painkiller John Snow (1813-59) introduced the scientific use of ether into English surgery. He administered chloroform to Queen Victoria during the birth of Prince Leopold in 1853, the first time it had ever been used on royalty, and again at the birth of Princess Beatrice in 1857. He lived at 18 SACKVILLE STREET, Piccadilly (house demolished in 1963) and is buried in BROMPTON CEMETERY, Earls Court [1F 75].

Rubber Plantation In 1876 Sir Henry Wickham, a British botanist, sent seeds of the Hevea rubber tree which he had collected in Brazil to the BOTANICAL GARDENS, KEW [1C 72]. Hundreds of these seedlings were sent to Ceylon and thus the rubber plantations of the Far East were established.

Rugby Football On or near the site of Canada House, Pall Mall East, stood the Pall Mall Restaurant where, on 26 January 1871, the Rugby Football Union was founded.

Running Footman On this tavern in HAY'S MEWS, Charles Street, Mayfair [4A 60c], hangs a sign which reads, 'I am the only Running Footman'. Formerly called the Running Horse, it was renamed in honour of the last running footman in Britain. Running footmen were employed to run ahead of coaches and warn innkeepers that their masters were approaching.

Ruskin, John (1819-1900) Writer. Born at 54 HUNTER STREET, St Pancras [4F 45] (house demolished 1970). He published works on art and aesthetics and was concerned with social and economic problems, making a number of social experiments. His works include *Modern Painters*, *The Seven Lamps of Architecture*, *The Stones of Venice* and *Sesame and Lilies*. Memorial in Poets' Corner, WESTMINSTER ABBEY.

Russell, Lord John (1792-1878) Liberal statesman. He entered Parliament in 1813 and was home secretary 1835-9, foreign secretary 1859-65 and prime minister 1846-52 and 1865-6. He supported Catholic emancipation and the Reform Bill. He lived at 37 CHESHAM PLACE, Belgrave Square [3F 62b].

Russian Eagle In Orme Square, Bayswater Road [2F 59], built in about 1815 and named after Mr Orme, the ground landlord, a column surmounted by a Russian eagle was erected to commemorate the victory over Napoleon. MOSCOW ROAD and ST PETERSBURG PLACE, Bayswater Road, both built in about 1815, were named in honour of the Czar's visit to London in 1814.

Russian Writer Alexander Herzen (1812-70), born in Moscow and exiled to Siberia for his political views, left Russia in 1847. In 1852 he came to London, where he set up a printing press and agitated for reforms in his country. He is famous for his *Memoirs*. He lived 1860-3 at 1 ORSETT TERRACE, Paddington [2A 60a].

S

Sadler's Wells Theatre, Rosebery Avenue [1A 61a] Named after Thomas Sadler, who owned the medicinal springs on the site. In 1683 he built a theatre and provided music for those who came to drink his water. The second and present theatre opened in 1931.

St Andrew-by-the-Wardrobe, Queen Victoria Street [3C 61a] The church derived its name from a nearby building in which the royal clothes were stored under the care of the Master of the King's Wardrobe, an office that ceased to exist in 1709. The church, rebuilt by Sir Christopher Wren after the fire of 1666, was damaged by bombs in the Second World War and has since been restored.

St James's Palace [1C 62c] Built by King Henry VIII on the site of a hospital for leprous maidens which was dedicated to St James the Less. From 1698 until 1837, this palace was the official residence of the sovereign, and all court functions were held here, but when Queen Victoria came to the throne the court moved to Buckingham Palace. The palace is the official home of the Poet Laureate and the Keeper of the Queen's Swans.

St John's Wood [4A-B 44] The home of Lord's Cricket Ground. Originally part of the Forest of Middlesex, it occupies the site of and takes its name from St John's Farm, demolished in about 1830, which was the property of the Priory of St John of Jerusalem.

St Martin-in-the-Fields, Trafalgar Square [4E 60d] As most of Buckingham Palace is in its parish the church is known as the Royal Parish Church. The present church, the third one on the site, was built 1721-6 from James Gibb's designs. It has a fine spire with a weather-vane adorned with a crown. George I was a church warden here, the only known instance of an English sovereign holding this office.

St Martins-le-Grand, Cheapside [3E 61b] On the site of the General Post Office stood a college of secular canons of St Martin le Grand, which gave the street its name. Granted a charter by William the Conqueror, the college, founded in about 750 and demolished in 1547, claimed the privileges of sanctuary.

St. Pancras Station.

St Mary-le-Strand, Strand [3A 61a] There was known to be a church in existence here in 1147, and it is said that Thomas à Becket was once its rector. The stones of the old church were used for the rebuilding of Somerset House after the church was rebuilt for Queen Anne to James Gibbs's designs 1717 (*see main entry*). In 1750 it is claimed that Bonny Prince Charlie was admitted to the Church of England here. The church was bombed during the Second World War.

St Olave's, Hart Street, Tower Hill [4A 61c] A fifteenth-century church with a twelfth-century crypt, dedicated to St Olaf, king and patron saint of Norway, who was martyred in the ninth century. The gateway, which is adorned with skulls, prompted Charles Dickens to call the church 'St Ghastly Grim'. The church, which escaped the fire of 1666, was wrecked by bombing in 1941 and reconstructed in 1954.

St Pancras [3E 45] Thought to be named after a fourteen year old Phrygian nobleman, who was beheaded in Rome in AD 304, for his adherence to the Christian faith. Because of the early age at which he suffered martyrdom, he was regarded as the patron saint of children.

St Paul's Cathedral [3D 61b] Cathedral church of the diocese of London. The first recorded church on the site was built by Ethelbert, first Christian king of Kent, and during the course of the centuries it was several times destroyed by fire and rebuilt. The Gothic old St Paul's was finally burnt down in the fire of 1666, to be replaced by the present cathedral, built to the designs of Sir Christopher Wren (*see main entry*) from 1675-1710. The cathedral, built in Portland stone, has the largest church dome in the world after St Peter's in Rome. Both the high altar and the north transept were damaged by bombs in 1941.

St. Paul's Cathedral designed by Sir Christopher Wren.

St Thomas's Hospital [2F 62d] London's second oldest hospital which in 1552 succeeded a hospital thought to have originated in the Priory of St Mary Overy early in the twelfth century and believed to have stood on or near the site of Southwark Cathedral, London Bridge. From 1215 until 1862 the Hospital occupied the site of the Chapter House of Southwark Cathedral, St Thomas' Street, London Bridge. The hospital was first dedicated to St Thomas à Becket, but Edward VI rededicated it to St Thomas the Apostle. It remained at the Surrey Gardens Music Hall, Kennington from 1862 until June 21, 1871, when it opened its present quarters on Lambeth Palace Road, Westminster Bridge.

Salvation Rink William Booth (1829-1912) founded the Christian Mission in the Mile End Road in 1865, thirteen years later changing the name to the Salvation Army, which is now established in almost every country in the world. REGENT HALL, 275 OXFORD STREET (3F 60b), the west London headquarters of the Salvation Army, was formerly an ice rink and is therefore known by members of the organization as 'The Rink'. William Booth's monument in the Mile End Road marks the spot where he began his meetings.

Sanctuary [2D 62d]. Broad Sanctuary extends from Westminster Abbey to Victoria Street, and derives its name from a church building that gave criminals protection from the law. Within forty days the criminals, clothed in sackcloth, were taken before the coroner to admit their guilt. They were then allowed to leave the country, but on returning without a licence, if caught they would be executed. The privilege of sanctuary was abolished in the reign of James I.

Sargent, John Singer (1854-1925) Painter. Born in Florence of American parents. His best-known paintings are 'Carnation', 'Ellen Terry', 'Coventry Patmore' and 'Carmencita'. He lived from 1901 till his death at 31 TITE STREET, Chelsea [1C 76].

Savile Row, Regent Street [3B 60c] Now famous for its tailors, the street was built 1733-6 for Richard Boyle, third Earl of Burlington, who named it after his wife, Lady Dorothy Savile. BURLINGTON GARDENS and BOYLE STREET honour the family name.

Saxon Arch ALL HALLOWS BY THE TOWER, EAST-CHEAP [3F 61b] occupies the site of a Roman villa on which the Saxons built a church, perhaps as early as 675. The church, rebuilt from the thirteenth to fifteenth centuries, was badly bombed in the Second World

War. A seventh-century Saxon arch escaped the bombing, and an eleventh-century cross was unearthed when the rubble was being cleared. Samuel Pepys (*see main entry*) watched the Great Fire of 1666 from the tower of this church.

Scott, Captain Robert Falcon (1868-1912) Antarctic explorer. He commanded an expedition in the *Discovery* in 1901-4. In June 1910 he and his crew set out in the *Terra Nova* on the South Pole Expedition, hoping to be the first to reach the Pole, but they were forestalled by Amundsen, the Norwegian explorer. Scott perished with his companions on their return march to base. He lived at 56 OAKLEY STREET, Chelsea [1B 76]. Statue by his sculptress wife in WATERLOO PLACE, Pall Mall [4D 60d]. The *Discovery* is moored on VICTORIA EMBANKMENT [4F 60d].

Scottish Patriot Sir William Wallace (1270-1305), Scottish national hero, annihilated an English army in 1297 in the Battle of Stirling Bridge. A year later, he was defeated by Edward I (1239-1307) at Falkirk. Betrayed and captured, he was executed on 23 August 1305. There is a memorial to him on the outer wall of Bart's Hospital (*see Hospital*).

Seacoal Lane, Ludgate Hill [3C 61a] So named because barges on the Fleet River landed coal here.

Secret Submarines From 1940 until September 1945 Northways, a block of flats at COLLEGE CRESCENT, Swiss Cottage, was the secret headquarters of the British Submarine Service. Here, the Navy planned the offensives off the Norwegian coast and in the Mediterranean. The tenants of the flats were unaware of what happened and carried on with their normal duties.

Seething Lane, Tower Hill [3A 61c] Used to be an area

for trades such as glue-bottling and soap-making, where animal skins were boiled for processing. Because of the steaming and smelly vats it was called Seething Lane.

Selwyn, George Augustine (1809-78) Churchman. Born in CHURCH ROW, HAMPSTEAD [1A 44], and christened at ST JOHN'S, Hampstead which is also in Church Row. In 1829 he rowed for Cambridge in the first inter-university boat race. In 1841 he was consecrated first Bishop of New Zealand, where he travelled extensively and preached in Maori. In 1867 he was appointed Bishop of Lichfield. Selwyn College, Cambridge was founded in his memory.

Serpentine, Hyde Park [1D 62b] Created by Queen Caroline, wife of George II, in 1730. In 1816, Harriet, the first wife of Shelley the poet, drowned herself here. In 1825 a Mr Hunt drove a coach and four across the frozen Serpentine for a bet. The Lido was opened in 1930 by Mr George Lansbury, the minister of works. (*See also Hyde Park.*)

Seven Dials, Shaftesbury Avenue [3E 60d] The home of the Cambridge Theatre was completed in about 1710 to designs by Thomas Neal, Master of the Royal Mint and was called Seven Dials because seven streets converged on a column adorned with seven dials. The column and dials were removed in 1774 to Addlestone and in 1822 to Weybridge, Surrey. NEAL STREET, Shaftesbury Avenue, commemorates the builder's name.

Seven Sisters Road [1F 45-2D 31] Runs from Holloway Road to High Road, Tottenham. It is said to have derived its name from The Seven Sisters tavern in Tottenham. There is a tradition that in front of it grew seven elms in a circle with a walnut tree in the centre.

Shackleton, Sir Ernest Henry (1874-1922) Irish-born explorer, educated at Dulwich College, who accompanied Scott on his 1901-4 expedition. In 1908 he sailed from New Zealand and got within a hundred miles of the South Pole. On his last expedition he died at sea. He lived at 12 WESTWOOD HILL, Lewisham [1B 108]. Statue outside the ROYAL GEOGRAPHICAL SOCIETY, KENSINGTON GORE, Kensington [2B 62a].

Shaw, George Bernard (1856-1950) Irish-born journalist and playwright who came to London in 1876 and was at first well known as a Fabian. His best-known plays are *Saint Joan*, *Candida*, *Major Barbara* and *Pygmalion*. He lived 1887-98 at 29 FITZROY SQUARE, Bloomsbury [1B 60c].

Shepherd's Well This ancient conduit which stood near the junction of FITZJOHN'S AVENUE and AKENSIDE ROAD, Hampstead [1A 44] used to be the main water supply for the local residents and gave employment to the poor, who sold it by the bucket. Late in the eighteenth century Lord Loughborough tried to close the well, but failed when the people took him to court. The well dried up in about 1870.

Sheraton, Thomas (1751-1806) One of England's foremost furniture makers and designers. He came to London in 1790. He wrote a number of theological and religious works as well as the *Cabinet Maker's and Upholsterer's Drawing Book* and the *Cabinet Dictionary*. He lived at 163 WARDOUR STREET, Soho [3C 60c]. SHERATON STREET, off Wardour Street, commemorates his name.

Sheridan, Richard Brinsley (1751-1816) Irish-born dramatist, manager of the Drury Lane Theatre in 1776. He wrote *The Rivals*, *The School for Scandal* and *The Critic*. Member of Parliament 1780-1812. Lived

1795-1802 at 10 HERTFORD STREET, Park Lane [1A 62c], and from 1813 until he died at 14 SAVILE ROW, Mayfair [3B 60c]. At Savile Row he had a special window made, enabling him to see his creditors when they called without himself being seen.

Sheriffs On Midsummer Day the City Guild elects two sheriffs at the GUILDHALL. This office, which can be held only once in a lifetime, came into being in the seventh century and is the oldest office in the City of London.

Shopping Arcades The ROYAL OPERA ARCADE, Pall Mall [1D 60d], a forerunner of the present-day shopping precinct, was built by John Nash in 1817. BURLINGTON ARCADE, Piccadilly [1A 62c], was erected in 1819 on the garden of Burlington House, residence of the Earl of Burlington. It is said that the earl, annoyed that people were using the garden as a rubbish dump, gave orders for the arcade to be built.

Siddons, Sarah (1755-1831) A great tragic actress who became famous for her impersonations of Lady Macbeth and other Shakespearian characters. Buried in ST MARY'S, PADDINGTON GREEN, Harrow Road [1B 60a]. Statue in forecourt of the same church.

Sister Agnes When the South African War broke out in 1899 a Miss Agnes Keyser and her sister Fanny who lived at 17 GROSVENOR CRESCENT, Hyde Park Corner [2F 62b], asked King Edward, then Prince of Wales, what they could do to help. He suggested that the sick and wounded officers be nursed in their house. The hospital was opened in December 1899 and became permanent. In 1941 the hospital was bombed, and four months later Sister Agnes died. In 1948 it moved to BEAUMONT STREET, Marylebone [1F 60b], where it was opened by Queen Mary as the King Edward VII Hospital for officers.

Sixpenny Man The term 'sixpenny man' refers to the daily rate of pay of a non-commissioned officer in the CHELSEA ROYAL HOSPITAL (*see main entry*), during the early part of the eighteenth century. John Carley (*d.*1777), who was married twice, is buried with both his wives in the old cemetery of the Hospital. The wording on his gravestone which can be seen through the railings in Royal Hospital Road, Chelsea, states that, 'He was a Sixpenny Man' of the Hospital.

Sloane, Sir Hans (1660-1753) Physician. He founded the Chelsea Physic Gardens in the Royal Hospital Road. His collections of art, books, etc., were purchased by the government and placed in Montague House (British Museum). He was secretary to the Royal Society 1693-1712 and in 1712 was created a baronet, the first physician in the country to receive this title. Pioneered a national health service for the poor. SLOANE SQUARE, SLOANE STREET, HANS CRESCENT, HANS PLACE and HANS STREET [2E 62b] were part of his estate and named in his honour. He lived 1695-1742 at 2 BLOOMSBURY PLACE, Bloomsbury [2E 60d], where he kept most of his collections.

Smallest ST ETHELBURGA'S, BISHOPSGATE [2A 61b], which was erected in about 1420 and escaped the Great Fire of 1666, is the smallest church in the City of London.

10 HYDE PARK PLACE, Bayswater Road [3D 60b], 5ft wide, is thought to be the smallest house in London.

Some of the patrons of THE NAG'S HEAD in KINNERTON STREET, Knightsbridge [2E 62b], claim that it is London's smallest tavern.

Smithfield [2C 61a] The 'smooth field', now one of the world's largest meat markets, was the principal cattle and horse market from the middle of the twelfth century until 1855. The annual BARTHOLOMEW FAIR (*see main entry*) used to be held here in August. The area, once a tournament ground for knights, was also the chief place of execution from the twelfth century and a number of Protestants were burned at the stake in the reign of Bloody Mary. Wat Tyler was slain here in 1381 in front of Richard II.

Smith Square, Millbank [3E 62d] Laid out early in the eighteenth century, it commemorates the name of its builder Sir James Smith. Because it contains the headquarters of the Labour Party, the Transport Workers' Union, the Conservative Party and, until 1970, the Liberal Party, it is known as the Political Square. (*See also Footstool Church.*)

Smollet Tobias (1721-1771) Novelist, trained as a surgeon. In 1759, he was imprisoned in the King's Bench Prison, Southwark, for writing a libellous article in the *Critical Review*. His best-known works are *Roderick Random*, *Peregrine Pickle* and *Humphrey Clinker*. He lived 1749-65 at 6 LAWRENCE STREET, Chelsea [1B 76].

Smuts, Jan (1870-1950) South African statesman and field marshal. During the Boer War, he was in command of the Boer forces, but afterwards worked for reconciliation with Britain. South African defence minister 1910-20, and prime Minister 1919-24 and 1939-48. He made a great contribution towards the Allies' war effort. Statue by the sculptor Jacob Epstein in PARLIAMENT SQUARE.

Snuff Makers Fribourg and Treyer, snuff-makers, of 34 HAYMARKET [4D 60d], were established in 1720 by Peter Fribourg on their present site. Their ledger goes back to 1764 and shows that they sold snuff to George II, George IV, Pitt, and Beau Brummel.

Soane Museum [2F 60d] Sir John Soane (1753-1837), architect of the Bank of England, presented to the nation his house at 13 LINCOLN'S INN FIELDS (*see main entry*), which he had designed for himself, together with his collections of art and antiquities. The house, together with Nos. 12 and 14, is now the Sir John Soane Museum, the contents still being as far as possible as Soane left them. Statue of Soane outside the BANK OF ENGLAND.

'Soapsuds Island' In the nineteenth century LATIMER ROAD, Shepherds Bush [1C 58], was noted for its many laundries, which is why it became known as 'Soapsuds Island'. Similarly, Acton was once called the 'Land of Laundries'.

Soho The area may have taken its name from the cry of the followers of the Duke of Monmouth (1649-85), who lived here. SOHO SQUARE [2D 60d] was laid out in the reign of Charles II. Originally called King's Square, but it later became Monmouth Square, taking its new name from the residence of the Duke of Monmouth. The Duke, Charles II's natural son, tried to seize the throne from James II, but was defeated and captured at Sedgmoor and later executed at the Tower. Soho, is now famous for its foreign shops, restaurants and nightclubs.

Somerset House, Strand [3F 60d] Takes its name from and occupies the site of a palace begun in 1547 by the Duke of Somerset, the Lord Protector, who was executed in 1552. It passed into the hands of the Crown, and became the home of Queen Elizabeth. The present building was built in three stages, the south front 1776-86 by Sir William Chambers, the east wing (now King's College) 1828-34 by Sir Robert Smirke and the west wing 1854-6 by Sir James Pennethorne. The palace is now occupied by government offices, including the Registrar General of Births, Marriages and Deaths.

Song and Dance London's first palais de danse, the HAMMERSMITH PALAIS in SHEPHERD'S BUSH ROAD [4C 58], was opened in 1919 by a Mr Booker and a Mr Mitchell. In 1938 it had the distinction of being the first dance hall to be televised. In 1946 the 'Write a Tune' contest was held here with the public acting as the judges; the contest was created to discover unknown British songwriters and the winning tune was 'Cruising Down the River'.

Soundproof Thomas Carlyle (*see main entry*), author of *The French Revolution*, in 1853 had double walls erected in his study at 24 CHEYNE ROW, Chelsea [1B 76], because he needed to work in silence. This is thought to have been the first fully soundproof room.

South Bank Arts On the South Bank, over Waterloo Bridge [4F 60d], are the ROYAL FESTIVAL HALL for concerts (built for the 1951 Festival of Britain and with, some claim, the most perfect acoustics in the world), two smaller concert halls—the PURCELL ROOM and the QUEEN ELIZABETH HALL (opened in 1967), the HAYWARD GALLERY (opened in 1968, for Arts Council exhibitions) and the NATIONAL FILM THEATRE (under the arch of Waterloo Bridge). The NATIONAL THEATRE is also being built nearby (at present it is temporarily in the Old Vic Theatre, Waterloo Road).

South Kensington Museums [3 B-C 62a] The SCIENCE MUSEUM, established in 1857, occupies a building in Exhibition Road built in 1928 and extended in 1963; it covers all aspects of science in technology and industry.

The GEOLOGICAL MUSEUM, just south of the Science Museum in the Exhibition Road, was first opened in

1837 and moved to its present quarters in 1935.

The NATURAL HISTORY MUSEUM, in the Cromwell Road, started with the collections of Sir Hans Sloane and Sir Joseph Banks (*see main entries*) to which further additions were made. The collections moved in 1881 to the present museum built 1873-80 by Alfred Waterhouse. The museum deals with animal and plant life, past and present.

The VICTORIA AND ALBERT MUSEUM, Cromwell Road, was founded in 1852 (under the inspiration of Prince Albert) and moved to its present site in 1857. It now occupies a building designed by Sir Aston Webb and completed in 1909. It exhibits the fine and applied arts of all countries and all periods.

Southwark Cathedral [1E 63b] Tradition has it that the first church on this site was established in about 606. Until 1540 it was dedicated to St Mary Overy ('over the river'). In 1106 Augustinian canons erected a large Norman church, which was burnt down in 1206 and replaced by a Gothic building. In 1540 the church was dedicated instead to St Saviour (taking its name from a small parish church nearby). The nave was restored in 1890-7 but the church still contains Norman remains, an Early English Lady Chapel, an altar screen of 1520 and the Harvard Chapel.

Soviet Fair Soviet Russia's first London trade exhibition was opened by the prime minister, Mr Macmillan, on 7 July 1961 at the Earls Court Stadium. Four days later Major Yuri Gagarin, the first man to enter space, paid a visit to the exhibition.

Spencer, Herbert (1820-1903) Philosopher. He worked as sub-editor of *The Economist* and later devoted his time to philosophical study and writing. His published works include *Social Statics*, *Education*, *First Principles* and *Principles of Sociology*. He lived

1866-87 at 35 QUEENS GARDENS, Lancaster Gate [3A 60a].

Spencer Street, Goswell Rd., Clerkenwell [4B 46] Commemorates the name of Sir John Spencer, Lord Mayor of London, whose daughter married the Royalist Lord Compton, Earl of Northampton. In 1643 she had the courage to attend to her husband's needs during the fighting at the Battle of Edgehill. Nearby Northampton Square commemorates the earl's name.

Spitalfields, Commercial Street [1B 61c] Noted for its fruit and vegetable market, founded in 1682. It derives its name from the Priory and Hospital of St Mary's Spital, founded in 1197 by Mr and Mrs Walter Brune. Many French Huguenot weavers who were expelled from their native land in 1685 made Spitalfields their home, as is indicated by the name WEAVER STREET, off nearby Buxton Street.

Squatters People who take over empty houses without permission and live in them. In June 1969 Conservative-controlled Lewisham was the first London borough to grant official recognition to a family squatting advisory association.

'Stage Doors' The archways that lead to Platform 1 at Waterloo Station and Platforms 16 and 17 at Victoria Station are known by passengers and old cab drivers alike as the 'stage doors'.

Standard on Cornhill This was a conduit with four spouts erected in 1582. It stood at the junction of BISHOPSGATE, CORNHILL, GRACECHURCH STREET and LEADENHALL STREET [3F 61b], which was then the centre of the City of London. Although the water ceased to flow in 1600, distances were measured from this standard to towns throughout the country.

Stanhope, Charles, third Earl (1753-1816) Reformer and inventor. He married the sister of William Pitt the Younger (*see main entry*) and invented an iron printing-press and a microscopic lens, both of which bear his name. Lived at 20 MANSFIELD STREET, Portland Place [2A 60c].

Staple Inn Hall, High Holborn [2A 61a] In the fourteenth century it was a hostel for wool merchants ('merchants of the staple'). In the fifteenth century it became an Inn of Chancery which it remained until 1884. The present building, which dates from the sixteenth century, was badly damaged by a flying bomb in August 1944 and rebuilt in its original style in 1955, incorporating some of the salvaged materials.

Steele's Road, Hampstead [2C 44] Commemorates Sir Richard Steele (1672-1729), essayist and dramatist. He founded the *Tatler* and collaborated with Joseph Addison on the *Spectator*. His plays include *The Tender Husband* and *The Conscious Lovers*. The house in Haverstock Hill where he lived in 1712 was demolished in 1867.

Stephen, Sir Leslie (1823-1904) Literary figure and father of Virginia Woolf, the novelist. Educated at King's College, Strand, editor of the *Cornhill* magazine and *The Dictionary of National Biography*. He lived at 22 HYDE PARK GATE, Kensington [2A 62a].

Stinking Lane The name unofficially given to KING EDWARD STREET, City [2D 61b], because it was used as a dumping ground for waste from the nearby Smithfield Market slaughterhouses and Newgate Market.

Stores' Festival London's first festival of stores began on 20 May 1968 and lasted for a fortnight. The festival was promoted by thirty of the large stores, whose aim was to demonstrate that London was the best shopping centre in the world. On the eve of its opening a parade was held in Hyde Park, at which Princess Alexandra, the royal patron of the festival, took the salute, accompanied by the Mayor of Westminster.

Stow, John (1525-1605) Historian, author of the *Survey of London*, published in 1598. He is buried in ST ANDREW UNDERSHAFT, ST MARY AXE [3A 61c], and every year on about 5 April, the day on which he died penniless, a service is held there attended by the Lord Mayor.

Street Market The few stalls left in STRUTTON GROUND, Victoria Street [3D 62d], are the remains of the oldest street market in the country. The street is named after Lord Stourton, whose town residence stood here.

Street of Lamps PRINCE CONSORT ROAD [2B 62a], leading to the southern entrance of the Albert Hall (*see main entry*) was built in 1887 and named after Prince Albert, Queen Victoria's husband. It is called the 'Street of Many Lamps', because there is a lamp post every few yards. Apparently a titled lady's three-year-old son was once killed by a hansom cab in the badly lit road. Determined that no other child should suffer the same fate, she had the lamp posts built. In July 1972, the gas lamps in this street were converted to electricity.

Strike The first recorded strike in the building trade was that at ST LEONARD'S CHURCH, SHOREDITCH [4D 47], which was rebuilt in about 1740 by George Dance the Elder (*see main entry*). The old stocks and whipping post are still preserved in the churchyard.

Suicides' Burial Up to 1823 it was the custom to bury a suicide at a crossroads within the parish where he lived. In June of that year a young man who committed suicide was buried at the junction of Hobart Place, Grosvenor Place and Grosvenor Gardens, near the rear entrance of BUCKINGHAM PALACE. This incident apparently annoyed George IV, so on 8 July the practice was abolished by Parliament.

Sullivan, Sir Arthur (1842-1900) Born in Lambeth, organist at ST MICHAEL'S, CHESTER SQUARE, Belgravia [3A 62c], from 1871-96. Collaborated with W. S. Gilbert (*see main entry*) on a series of comic operas, of which the most celebrated are *The Pirates of Penzance*, *The Gondoliers* and *The Mikado*. They were all produced at the Savoy Theatre, Strand. He lived at 58 VICTORIA STREET [3B 62c]. Buried in ST PAUL'S CATHEDRAL. Bust on VICTORIA EMBANKMENT [3B 61a].

Surrey Jail On the site of the Weights and Measures Office in HARPER ROAD (formerly Horsemonger Lane), Borough High Street [2D 63b], stood the Horsemonger Lane County Jail of Surrey from 1798-1878. Leigh Hunt (*see main entry*), imprisoned for libel, was visited there by Byron and Tom Moore. It was after witnessing a hanging there that Charles Dickens began agitation for the abolition of public executions.

Suspension Bridge The original HAMMERSMITH BRIDGE [1B 74], constructed in 1827 by William Tierney Clark (1783-1852), was the first bridge in Greater London to be erected on the suspension principle. The present suspension bridge by Bazalgette, incorporating parts of the original one, was opened in 1887 by Prince Albert, Duke of Clarence.

'Swedish Nightingale', The Jenny Lind or Johanna Maria Lind (1820-87), Swedish soprano born in

Stockholm, made her first appearance in London in 1847 at the Haymarket Theatre, where she was received with great enthusiasm. In 1852 she married her accompanist, Otto Goldschmidt. From 1883-6 she was a professor of singing at the Royal College of Music. She lived 1874-87 in the BOLTONS, Old Brompton Road [4A 62a]. Memorial in WESTMINSTER ABBEY.

Sweep's Church ST GEORGE THE MARTYR, QUEEN SQUARE, Bloomsbury [1F 60d], erected 1706-23, was one of the churches built for Queen Anne. In the eighteenth century a charity provided a hundred apprentice sweeps of London and Westminster with a free Christmas dinner, and so the church came to be known as the Sweeps' Church.

Swinburne, Algernon Charles (1837-1909) He and Dante Gabriel Rossetti (*see main entry*) were attacked as being leaders of the 'fleshy school of poetry'. His best-known works are 'Atalanta in Calydon', 'The Garden of Persephone' and 'A Foresaken Garden'. He lived at 16 CHEYNE WALK, Chelsea [1A 76].

Synagogue After the resettlement of the Jews under Oliver Cromwell, the Spanish and Portuguese erected their first synagogue in 1657 in CREECHURCH LANE, Aldgate [3A 61c]. It was demolished in 1701 and in the same year rebuilt in nearby BEVIS MARKS, Houndsditch.

T

Tachbrook Street [4C 62c] This little street market, off the Vauxhall Bridge Road, takes its name from the nearby River Tachbrook which has now been converted into a storm sewer.

Tate Gallery, Millbank [4E 62d] The national collection of British art, built partly on the site of Millbank Penitentiary (*see main entry*), opened in August 1897. It is named after Sir Henry Tate (1819-99), the sugar refiner, who gave £80,000 and his own collection of paintings. The original building was designed by Sidney R. J. Smith and further galleries have since been added. The gallery contains works by almost every important British painter since the seventeenth century and a number of contemporary foreign works.

Taxis In 1634 Captain Bailey of Hackney was allowed to put four carriages to apply for hire outside St Mary-le-Strand in the Strand. Two hundred years later, in 1834, Mr J. Hansom of Birmingham invented the hansom cab. On 23 March 1907 seventeen motor-driven cabs left the General Motor Cab Company Garage (now the London General Cab Company Limited) at 1-3 Brixton Road, Brixton. These, the first motor taxis, were fitted with a taximeter—a clockwise device linked to the wheels and showing the distance and the fare—hence the term 'taxi-cabs'.

Television The first practical demonstration of the technique was staged by John Logie Baird in 1926 at

22 Frith Street, Soho. *Here Looking At You* with Leslie Mitchell, the first public transmission, was relayed from ALEXANDRA PALACE (*see main entry*) on 26 August 1936. Regular transmissions began on 2 November in the same year. The BBC in WOOD LANE, White City [2C 58], occupying thirteen acres, is the largest television headquarters in Europe.

Temple Bar, Fleet Street [3A 61a] There has been a gateway at this point, marking the entrance to the City from Westminster, since the twelfth century. The one built by Wren in 1672 was removed in 1878 to Theobalds' Park, Herts. The present memorial, erected in 1880, bears statues of Queen Victoria and Edward VII (then Prince of Wales) and is adorned with a griffin. Originally the heads of executed criminals were exposed on spikes on top of the gateway. When the sovereign visits the City on state occasions he or she receives the sword of state from the Lord Mayor and returns it before entering the City.

Thackeray, William Makepeace (1811-63) Educated at Charterhouse School. In 1846, he moved to 16 YOUNG STREET, Kensington [3F 59], where he wrote *Vanity Fair*, *Pendennis* and *Henry Esmond*. Later he edited the *Cornhill Magazine*. He lived 1853-9 at PUMP COURT, Middle Temple, Strand [4A 64], and died at 2 PALACE GREEN, Kensington [3F 59], buried in KENSAL GREEN CEMETARY.

Theatres James Burbage (*d.*1597), actor, felt that the City Corporation was biased against actors; so, in 1576, he built London's first theatre on the site of Nos. 86 and 88, CURTAIN ROAD, Old Street [1A 61c], then outside the city wall, and called it the Theatre. In 1598 the theatre, which was made of wood, was taken down in a single night by his two sons because there was a dispute about the lease. The materials were used for the Globe Theatre in Southwark. In 1596 Burbage also reopened the Blackfriars Playhouse (first opened 1576), which is remembered in the name PLAYHOUSE YARD, Blackfriars [3C 61a]. He is buried in ST LEONARD'S CHURCH, Shoreditch [4D 47].

Theatre Censorship A political satire, *The Historical Register*, staged at the Haymarket Theatre in 1736, contained a caricature of Sir Robert Walpole (*see main entry*), the prime minister, under the name of 'Quidam'. His outraged reaction led to the passing of an Act bringing plays under the censorship of the Lord Chamberlain. Stage censorship was abolished in 1968.

Theobalds Road, Bloomsbury [1F 60d] So named because it led to Theobalds in Hertfordshire, the favourite hunting resort of James I, son of Mary Queen of Scots.

Three Crowns Queen Caroline, wife of George II, once asked Sir Robert Walpole what he estimated it would cost to enclose the three royal parks for the exclusive use of the Court. 'Madam, the price would be three crowns, those of England, Ireland and Scotland,' was the minister's answer.

Through Space Many Londoners can claim to travel through space. If they travel east-west along the King's Road, Chelsea [2F 75-4E 62b], they pass The Man in the Moon, The Globe and reach The World's End. All three are taverns.

Tower Bridge [1B 63c] One of the famous landmarks of London. Built by the City Corporation from designs by Sir Horace Jones and Sir John Wolfe Barry and opened on 30 June 1894. Before the bridge opens to enable larger vessels to sail through a bell is rung to warn pedestrians and traffic. In December 1952, as

London's famous Tower Bridge.

the bridge was going up, a bus leapt the gap and landed safely on the other side; twelve passengers and the conductor were taken to hospital with injuries.

Tower of London [4B 61c] William the Conqueror first built what is now known as the WHITE TOWER as a fortress to protect the city, control the approaches and impress the citizens. Over the centuries different monarchs made further additions and alterations and the Tower has been variously used as a royal palace, a state prison, a museum, a mint, a treasury, an observatory and even a royal zoo (until 1834 the Lion Tower contained a royal menagerie). The Tower is garrisoned by a Constable and Yeoman Warders, ex-servicemen who will show visitors around. The White Tower, the oldest part of the fortress, now contains a collection of arms and armour and the CHAPEL OF ST JOHN, the oldest church in London. In the BLOODY TOWER it is believed that the two little princes, nephews of Richard III (*r.*1483-5), were murdered and Sir Walter Raleigh was imprisoned here for thirteen years. A brass plate on TOWER GREEN marks the site of the scaffold where those of royal or noble blood were executed, among them Anne Boleyn and Catherine Howard, wives of Henry VIII. Traitors'

Gate was the gateway through which so many prisoners passed when they came by water from Westminster. More cheerfully, the CROWN JEWELS (*see main entry*) can be inspected in a stronghold specially constructed to house them.

Tower Ravens Legend has it that if the ravens at the TOWER OF LONDON were to disappear completely, through death or flight, the Tower would be invaded and the Commonwealth would expire. The ravens are looked after by one of the Beefeaters known as the Raven Master, who ensures that their wings are clipped every three months.

Trafalgar Square [4D 60d] Laid out in 1829-41 by Sir Charles Barry and named after Nelson's victory at Trafalgar in 1805. NELSON'S COLUMN (*see main entry*) overlooks the square.

Traffic Computers Traffic was computerized for the first time in the country in Westminster, Chelsea and Kensington on 22 January 1968. More than a hundred sets of traffic lights covering seventy intersections were linked to two computers at Scotland Yard.

Trenchard, Hugh Montague, first viscount (1873-1956) In 1914 he was appointed officer in charge of the Royal Flying Corps and was responsible for air operations in the First World War. On the formation of the Royal Air Force, he became Chief of Staff. He served as Commissioner of the Metropolitan Police 1931-5. Buried in WESTMINSTER ABBEY. Statue in VICTORIA GARDENS, Victoria Embankment [4F 60d].

Trinity Church This church, which was built in 1822 when Trinity Church Square, Borough High Street [2E 63b], was laid out by the Corporation of Trinity

House, was closed in 1959. Early in 1900 it was popularized by Tom Costello, Music Hall artist, in his song 'Trinity Church I met My Doom'.

Trollope, Anthony (1815-82) Novelist. Educated at Harrow, worked as a civil servant for the Post Office. His best-known novels are probably *Barchester Towers, Dr Thorne, The Small House at Allington* and *The Last Chronicles of Barset*. He lived 1873-80 at 39 MONTAGU SQUARE, Marylebone [2E 60b], and died at 34 WELBECK STREET [2A 60c]. Buried in KENSAL GREEN CEMETERY.

Tube Church ST MARY WOOLNOTH above the BANK tube station [3E 61b] dates back to the twelfth century and was rebuilt by Nicholas Hawksmoor in 1716-27. It is the only church in London to have trains running underneath it: in 1900, the year the line opened, the crypt of the church was removed and replaced with a booking hall and lift shafts.

Tuppeny Tube The original Central Line, Shepherds Bush to Bank, was opened in July 1900 and was called the Tuppeny Tube because the fare was a uniform 2d. On 1 July 1907 the fare was raised for journeys of more than eight stations. The present line, running from West Ruislip to Epping, just under 34¼ miles, is the longest tube line in the world.

Turner, Joseph Mallord (1775-1851) Eccentric, unmarried landscape painter. Born in MAIDEN LANE [4E 60d], baptized in the nearby ST PAUL'S, COVENT GARDEN. 'The Calais Pier', 'Shipwreck' and 'Burial at Sea' are among his famous paintings. He lived at 37 QUEEN ANNE STREET, HARLEY STREET [2A 60c]. Died at 118 CHEYNE WALK, Chelsea [1A 76]. Buried in ST PAUL'S CATHEDRAL.

Twain, Mark (1830-1910) The pen name of Samuel Langhorne Clemens, the American writer, who first worked as printer, Mississippi pilot and goldminer. He wrote *Innocents Abroad*, *Huckleberry Finn* and *Tom Sawyer*. He first came to England in 1875 and returned 1896-7 when he lived at 23 TEDWORTH SQUARE, Chelsea [1C 76].

Tyburn Gallows Near the present site of MARBLE ARCH, at the foot of the Edgware Road [3E 60b], many condemned prisoners from NEWGATE PRISON or the TOWER OF LONDON paid the final penalty. The first execution was in 1196, the last in 1783, and from 1571 till 1759 there was a permanent gallows known as Tyburn Tree. Among the people executed here were the highwaymen Jonathan Wild, Claude Duval and Jack Sheppard.

U

United Service Club, Pall Mall [1C 62c] Built in 1827 from Nash's designs and remodelled in 1842, it is called 'The Senior' because when it was founded in 1815 it was only for officers not below the rank of major. In 1892 lower ranking officers were admitted. The gas-fed flambeaux attached to the building are lit up for state visits, Battle of Britain day, Trafalgar day and Waterloo day.

University Steam Locomotive Attached to the wall of UNIVERSITY COLLEGE, GOWER STREET [1D 60d], is a memorial tablet to Richard Trevithick (1771-1833), pioneer of high pressure steam, who ran the first steam engine to draw passenger carriages 'close to this place' in 1808.

V

Vaccination Dr Edward Jenner (1749-1823), a pupil of John Hunter (*see main entry*), discovered vaccination against smallpox and made his first innoculation in 1796. His practice was opposed by the public and a number of scientists, but in 1853 vaccination was made compulsory in this country. In 1804 he lived at 4 Hertford Street, Mayfair [1A 62c]. Statue by the Long Water, Kensington Gardens.

Vale of Health, East Heath Road, Hampstead [4A 28] Reputed to have got its name from the local supply of pure well water. It is maintained that this was the reason why everyone living here in 1665 escaped the plague.

Victoria Falls David Livingstone (1813-73), Scottish missionary and explorer, first worked in a cotton mill and then became a doctor. In 1840 he went to Africa where he discovered the Victoria Falls and was the first European to travel the entire length of Lake Tanganyika. In 1871 he was joined by Stanley who uttered the famous greeting: 'Dr Livingstone I presume'. Buried in Westminster Abbey. Statue outside the Royal Geographical Society, Kensington Gore [2B 60a].

Villiers Street, Strand [4E 60d] Honours the name of George Villiers, first duke of Buckingham (1592-1630), a favourite of James I, whose town house stood here. It was sold in 1672 by the second duke, who made the stipulation that the new streets should bear the family name and titles—hence too nearby BUCKINGHAM STREET.

Voltaire (1694-1778) The name assumed by François-Marie Arouet, French writer. He was twice imprisoned in the Bastille and finally established himself at Ferney, near Geneva. His works include *Zadig*, *Candide*, *Lettres Philosophiques sur les Anglais* and the plays *Merope* and *Irene*. He visited London 1726-9 and lived in MAIDEN LANE, Covent Garden [4E 60d].

W

Walpole, Sir Robert, first earl of Orford (1676-1745) Whig statesman. He entered Parliament in 1701 and was secretary for war 1708-10, treasurer of the Navy 1710, and first lord of the treasury and chancellor of the exchequer 1715-7 and 1721-42. He lived from 1743 until his death at 5 Arlington Street, Piccadilly [4B 60c]. Generally reckoned to be the first prime minister in the modern sense, he lived at 10 Downing Street (*see main entry*) 1735-42. Walpole Street, Chelsea [4E 62b] indicates the site of his Chelsea residence.

Walworth [1B 78] For slaying the rebel Wat Tyler in Smithfield in 1381, the Mayor of London, Sir William Walworth, was rewarded by Richard II by having a district of Southwark named after him.

Washington, George (1732-99) Commander-in-chief of the American forces during the War of Independence, he was in 1789 elected first president of America and re-elected in 1793. His monument in Trafalgar Square was erected in 1921. There is also a bust in St. Paul's Cathedral.

Washington Inn During the latter half of the First World War a picturesque hut resembling a country inn was erected in the centre of St James's Square, Pall Mall [4b 60c]. The hut, demolished in 1921, was called the Washington Inn because it was used mainly by the American armed forces.

Watch House Attached to ST SEPULCHRE'S CHURCH, HOLBORN VIADUCT [2C 61a], is a watch house which was built in 1729 to survey the graveyard and keep away the professional body snatchers who sold the corpses to some of the surgeons attached to Bart's Hospital. It was destroyed by a bomb in 1941 and rebuilt in 1962.

Water Supply In 1613, Sir Hugh Myddleton (1560-1631), banker, goldsmith and clothmaker, initiated a new water supply system whereby a supply of pure water from the springs in Amwell, Hertfordshire was brought to Pentonville by a canal forty miles long. The course has since been shortened so that it ends at the pumping station at Green Lanes, near Manor House. AMWELL STREET [4A 46] off Rosebery Avenue and nearby MYDDLETON SQUARE commemorate Myddleton and his scheme. Statue in Islington Green, near the Angel.

Waterloo Bridge [4F 60d] The first Waterloo Bridge, built by John Rennie and opened in 1817, was demolished in 1936. The present one, designed by Sir Giles Gilbert Scott was first opened in 1942 but the official opening ceremony was held in December 1945. This was the first all-concrete bridge to be erected across the Thames.

Watts, Isaac (1674-1748) Nonconformist churchman. In 1702 he became minister to the Independent Church in Mark Lane, City. He wrote a number of hymns, including 'When I survey the wondrous cross' and 'O God, our help in ages past'. He lived the last thirty-six years of his life and died at Abney Park Mansion (now a cemetery), Stamford Hill [4D 31], where there is a monument to him. Buried in BUNHILL FIELDS, Moorgate. Monument in WESTMINSTER ABBEY.

Wax Works During the French Revolution, Madame Tussaud (1761-1850) was forced to take death masks from the guillotined heads and was herself thrown in prison. She came to London in 1802 and opened her exhibition at the Lyceum in the Strand. Later she transferred it to the Portman Rooms, Baker Street, where it remained until it moved to its present quarters in MARYLEBONE ROAD [1F 60b] in 1884. For the last nine years of her life Madame Tussaud lived nearby at 58 BAKER STREET.

'Wedding Cake' The Queen Victoria Memorial outside BUCKINGHAM PALACE was designed by Sir Aston Webb and sculptured by Sir Thomas Brock. On 16 May 1911 Sir Thomas Brock was made Knight Commander of the Bath by George V on the platform

The Queen Victoria Memorial.

of the memorial at the same time as the unveiling. Because of the monument's design, it is known by all London cabbies as 'the wedding cake'.

Wedding Cake Spire ST BRIDE'S, FLEET STREET [3B 61a], known to have been in existence as early as 1235 but gutted by the Great Fire of 1666, was rebuilt by Christopher Wren 1670-84 with a fine spire often known as 'the wedding cake spire'. In 1764 the spire 234ft high, was struck by lightning and rebuilt 8ft shorter. The church was reopened after bomb damage in 1957. It is popularly known as the 'parish church of the press', since it stands in Fleet Street.

Wellington, Arthur Wellesley, first Duke (1769-1852). Called the Iron Duke. Gave his name to the wellington boot. As one of England's greatest military commanders he led the British forces in the Peninsular War and in 1815 defeated Napoleon at Waterloo. He was Tory prime minister 1828-30. He lived at APSLEY HOUSE (*see main entry*), Hyde Park Corner. Statue outside the house and stirrupless equestrian statue outside the ROYAL EXCHANGE, City [3F 61b]. After his death he lay in state in the Great Hall of the CHELSEA ROYAL HOSPITAL before being buried in ST PAUL'S CATHEDRAL.

Wells, Herbert George (1866-1946) Novelist. He wrote novels of social comment such as *Kipps* and *The History of Mr Polly* and science-fiction works such as *The Time Machine* and *The Invisible Man*. He lived and died at 13 HANOVER TERRACE, Regent's Park [4B 44].

Wembley [1D 40] In April 1923 the stadium held its first football Cup Final (*see main entry*); the game between West Ham and Bolton Wanderers ended with the latter winning 2-0. Wembley again came into prominence during the British Empire exhibitions of 1924 and 1925, and in 1948 when the Olympic Games were held there.

West, Benjamin (1738-1820) American painter who came to London in 1761. His best-known paintings are 'Penn's Treaty with the Indians' and 'The Death of Wolfe'. In 1768 he was married at ST MARTIN-IN-THE-FIELDS, Trafalgar Square. In 1792 he was elected president of the Royal Academy. He lived and died at 14 NEWMAN STREET, Oxford Street [2b 60c].

Westminster Abbey [2E 62d] Officially called the Collegiate Church of St. Peter. A church was first built here in the seventh or eighth century on the site known as the Island of Thorney and was rebuilt by Edward the Confessor (*d.*1066) and consecrated in 1065. In the

Westminster Abbey, close to the Houses of Parliament. The Abbey has seen the Coronation of every English monarch since William the Conqueror in the eleventh century.

time of Henry III (1207-72) it was extensively rebuilt in the Early English style. Henry VII (1457-1509) added the chapel in the Tudor style which became his own burial-place. The west towers were built in 1740 by Wren's pupil, Nicholas Hawksmoor. The north transept was remodelled in 1884 by Sir George Gilbert Scott.

Since the time of William the Conqueror all coronations have taken place here; the CORONATION CHAIR was made in 1307 and incorporates the Stone of Scone, on which all Scottish kings had been crowned since 850. The Abbey is crowded with monuments to the famous dead—too many to list, but POETS' CORNER and the tomb of the Unknown Warrior are particularly notable. Many sovereigns are buried here (though not all, and none since George II in 1760).

Westminster Bridge [2F 62d] The first Westminster Bridge, the first bridge to be built across the Thames after London Bridge, opened in 1750 and was erected partly with money raised by public lottery and partly with government grants. The present one was opened in 1852. 85ft wide, it is one of the widest bridges in Europe.

Westminster Cathedral [3C 62c] Principal Roman Catholic church in England, seat of the Archbishop of Westminster. It was built 1895-1903 in the Byzantine style to the design of John Francis Bentley. The nave is the widest in England (60ft across) and can contain about 2,000 people. It is possible to go up the tower (284ft high) from which there is a fine view of London.

Westminster Hospital [3D 62d] Established in 1719 in Petty France, St. James's Park, it was the first hospital to depend on the voluntary support of the public. The hospital was rebuilt in 1834 in Broad Sanctuary (*see Main Entry Sanctuary*) and moved to its present site in HORSEFERRY ROAD, Millbank in 1939.

Whistler, James Abbott McNeil (1834-1903) American-born painter. He came to London in 1863 and 1866-78 lived at 96 CHEYNE WALK, Chelsea [1A 76], where he painted 'A Portrait of My Mother'. In 1878, the year he moved to 21 TITE STREET, Chelsea [1C 76], he was awarded a farthing damages in a libel action against Ruskin. He subsequently lived at 13 and 46 Tite Street. In 1890, he published his book *The Gentle Art of Making Enemies*. He died at 76 Cheyne Walk.

Whitechapel Mount In 1808 the Corporation of London cleared a huge dump, thought to have been rubble either from the old St Paul's Cathedral or from the trenches dug by anti-Royalists during the Civil War. With it they built EAST MOUNT STREET, near the London Hospital [2D-E 61d]. The dump, said to be 330ft long and 180ft wide, was known as the 'Whitechapel Mount'.

Whitecross Street, Old Street [4C 46] Presumed to have derived its name from a nearby stone cross. From 1813 until it was demolished in 1877 the Whitecross Street Prison, an establishment capable of housing 500 inmates, stood in this street.

White's Club At 37 ST JAMES'S STREET, Piccadilly [4B 60c], London's oldest club and once the chief Tory club. It was founded in 1693 by Francis White as a coffee house and became a club in 1736. It was noted in the eighteenth century for its wealthy gamblers.

Whittington, Sir Richard (1350-1427) Merchant and Lord Mayor. He donated large sums of money to St Thomas's and Bart's Hospitals, founded a library at the Greyfriars Monastery, Newgate Street, City, and built almshouses. He was Lord Mayor of London in 1396, 1397, 1406 and 1419. He lived in CRUTCHED FRIARS, near Tower Hill [4A 61c], and died in his house in COLLEGE HILL, Cannon Street [3E 61b], next door to ST MICHAEL'S PATERNOSTER ROYAL, where he is buried. (*see Highgate Hill*).

Widow's Son Legend has it that in 1824 the sailor son of a widow who kept an alehouse on the site of The Widow's Son tavern in DEVONS ROAD, Bow [1C 64], asked his mother to save him a hot cross bun for his homecoming from the sea. This she did, but her son disappeared and was never heard of again. Convinced that he would return his mother every Easter baked him some hot cross buns. In memory of this a bun is added to the tavern's collection every Easter.

Wig and Pen This club at 230 STRAND [4E 60d] was founded in 1947. Built in 1625 on Roman remains it was the only building in the Strand to escape the fire of 1666. On the day when the Lord Mayor of London is received at the Law Courts opposite by the Lord Chief Justice, all children and their parents are welcomed at the club, and all are presented with a gift.

Wilberforce, William (1759-1833) Reformer and Member of Parliament, from 1780 he devoted himself to the abolition of slavery and in 1807 saw his bill putting an end to the slave trade passed. Just before he died, he heard that all slaves in the Empire were to be set free. He lived at 44 CADOGAN PLACE, Sloane Street [2E 62b]. Buried in WESTMINSTER ABBEY.

Wilde, Oscar (1854-1900) Writer. After his novel, *The Picture of Dorian Gray*, he wrote such comedies as *Lady Windermere's Fan* and *The importance of Being Earnest*. He lived 1884-95 at 34 TITE STREET, Chelsea [1C 76].

William III (1650-1702) As Prince of Orange, he married Mary, daughter of James II, and at the opposition's invitation he invaded England and came to the throne in 1688 after his father-in-law fled to France. During his reign a Bill was passed making England a constitutional monarchy with Parliament in control of policy. He fell off his horse in Hampton Court and died from his injuries. Statue in ST JAMES'S SQUARE, Pall Mall [4C 60c].

Wolfe, James (1727-59) British general who distinguished himself in the battles of Culloden and Laffeldt. He was killed leading the British forces against the French at Quebec, but the victory was British and Canada became a British colony. Buried in ST ALPHEGE'S, Church St., Greenwich (*see Greenwich*). Statue in GREENWICH PARK, and monument in WESTMINSTER ABBEY. OLD QUEBEC STREET, Marble Arch [3E 60b], built in 1760, commemorates the victory of Quebec.

Wren, Sir Christopher (1632-1723) Architect. Educated at Westminster School, he studied mathematics and was a professor of astronomy before he turned his abilities to architecture. After the Great Fire of 1666 he built over fifty city churches, including ST PETER'S CORNHILL, ST BRIDE'S, Fleet Street, and ST MARY-LE-BOW, Cheapside. As well as his masterpiece, ST PAUL'S CATHEDRAL, he also designed the ROYAL EXCHANGE, MARLBOROUGH HOUSE and GREENWICH HOSPITAL, As Surveyor of Works, he lived in GREAT SCOTLAND YARD (*see main entry*), and during the building of St Paul's lived at Cardinal House, 50 BANKSIDE [4D 61b]. He is, appropriately, buried in St Paul's Cathedral.

Z

Zoo [3C 44] Officially entitled the Gardens of the Zoological Society of London, on the north side of REGENT'S PARK (*see main entry*). It was founded in 1826 by Sir Stamford Raffles and Sir Humphry Davy and opened in 1828. In 1831 the animals from the Tower of London royal menagerie were added to the Zoo, which now contains over seven thousand animals and is visited by about two million people each year.

Where to find it in Central London

Key to Maps

LANDMARKS

Admiralty Arch	VD1
Albert Hall	IV D2-3
Albert Memorial	IV D2
Centre Point	II D4
City Temple	III B4
Guildhall	III C4, V D2
Horse Guards	V D2
Inner Temple	VI A1
Mansion House	III C4 ,VI C1
Monument	VI D1
Nelson's Column	V D1
Royal Courts of Justice	II F4
Royal Hospital, Chelsea	V A4
Royal Mint	VI F1
Tower of London	VI E1

MUSEUMS AND COLLECTIONS

British Museum	II D3
Courtauld Institute Gallery	II D3
Geffrye Museum	III E1
Geological Museum	IV D3
Hayward Gallery	V F1
Imperial War Museum	VI A3
London Museum	IV B2
National Gallery	V D1
National Portrait Gallery	V D1
Natural History Museum	IV D3
Royal Academy	V C1
Science Museum	IV D3
Soane Museum	II F4
Tate Gallery	V D4
Victoria and Albert Museum	IV D3
Wallace Collection	II A4

RELIGIOUS BUILDINGS

St Paul's Cathedral	III B4

Southwark Cathedral	VI C1
Westminster Abbey	V D3
Westminster Cathedral	V C3

PALACES

Buckingham Palace	V B2-3
Kensington Palace	IV B2
Lambeth Palace	V F3
St James's Palace	V C2

STREETS AND SQUARES

Birdcage Walk	V CD2-3
Burlington Arcade	V C1
Carnaby Street	II C4
Constitution Hill	V B2
Haymarket	V D1
Hyde Park Corner	V A2
King's Road Chelsea	IV F4
Knightsbridge	IV EF2
Leicester Square	V D1
The Mall	V CD2
Minories	III E4
Oxford Street	II ABC4
Pall Mall	V C2
Park Lane	IV F1
Piccadilly	V BC1, 2
Piccadilly Circus	V C1
Printing House Square	III B4
Regent Street	V C1; II BC4
Rotten Row	IV DEF2
Savile Row	V C1
Shaftesbury Avenue	
Speaker's Corner	IV F1
Trafalgar Square	V D1

PARKS AND GARDENS

Hyde Park	IV E1
Kensington Gardens	IV BDE1-2

Primrose Hill	I F1
Regent's Park	II A1-2
St James's Park	V CD2

BRIDGES

Blackfriars Bridge	VI A1
Lambeth Bridge	V E3
London Bridge	VI D1
Southwark Bridge	VI C1
Tower Bridge	VI E1-2
Waterloo Bridge	V F1
Westminster Bridge	V E2

MARKETS

Billingsgate	VI D1
Borough	VI C2
Covent Garden	II E4
Leadenhall Market	III D4
Portobello Road	IV A1
Smithfield	III B3
Spitalfields Market	III E3

STATIONS

Cannon Street	VI C1
Charing Cross	V E1
Euston	II C2
King's Cross	II E1
Liverpool Street	III D3
Marylebone	I E4
Paddington	I D4
St Pancras	II D1
Victoria	V B3-4
Waterloo	V F2
West London Air Terminal	IV BC3

GOVERNMENT BUILDINGS

Admiralty	V D2
Central Hall	V D3

County Hall	V EF2
10 Downing Street	V D2
Foreign Office	V D2
Houses of Parliament	V E3
Treasury	V D2

PLACES OF ENTERTAINMENT

Coliseum	V D1
National Film Theatre	V F1
New National Theatre	V F1
Old Vic (National Theatre)	VI A2
Royal Festival Hall	V F2
Royal Opera House	II E4
Sadler's Wells Theatre	III A2

SHOPPING

Army and Navy Stores	V C3
Barkers	IV B3
Bourne and Hollingsworth	II C4
Dickins and Jones	II C4
Fortnum and Mason	V C1
Foyle's	II D4
Harrod's	IV F3
Heal's	II CB
Peter Jones	IV F4
John Lewis	II B4
Liberty's	II C4
Marshall and Snelgrove	II B4
Peter Robinson	II B4
Selfridge's	II A4

MISCELLANEOUS

The Albany	V C1
Apsley House	V A2
Bank of England	III D4
Broadcasting House (BBC)	II B3-4
Design Centre	V D1
George Inn, Southwark	VI C2

Grand Union Canal	III BC1
Lincoln's Inn Fields	II F4
'Little Venice'	I C3
Lords Cricket Ground	I D2
Madame Tussaud's	II A3
Planetarium	II A3
Post Office Tower	II C3
Regent's Canal	II DEF1
St Katherine Docks	VI F1
Scotland Yard	V E1-2
Seymour Hall	I EF4
Sotheby's	V B1
Student Centre	II D3-4
Zoological Gardens (Zoo)	II A1

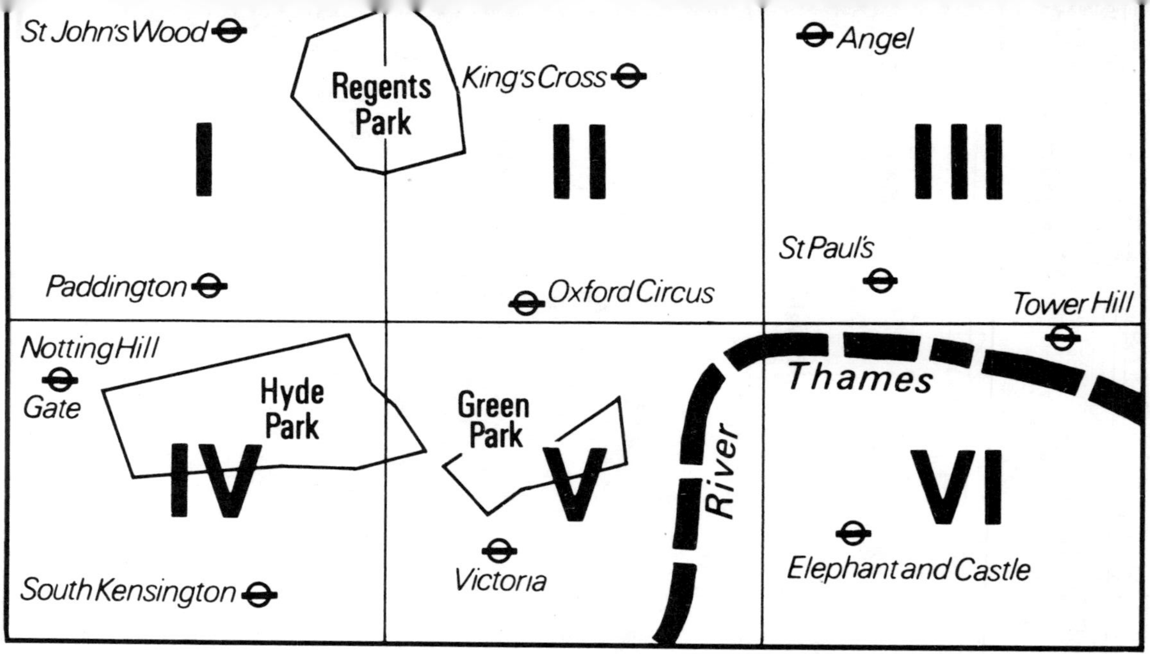
St John's Wood
Regents Park
King's Cross
Angel
I
II
III
Paddington
Oxford Circus
St Paul's
Tower Hill
Notting Hill Gate
Hyde Park
Green Park
Thames
River
IV
V
VI
Victoria
Elephant and Castle
South Kensington

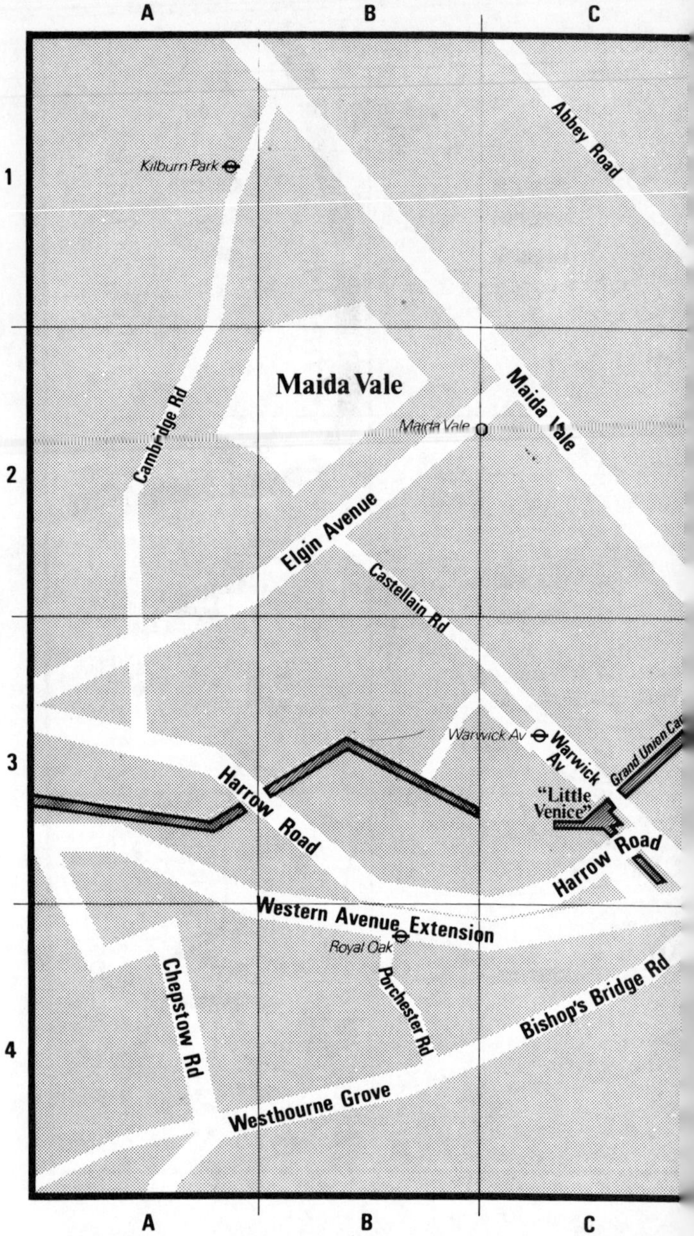

A
B
C
1
2
3
4
Kilburn Park
Abbey Road
Maida Vale
Cambridge Rd
Maida Vale
Maida Vale
Elgin Avenue
Castellain Rd
Warwick Av
Warwick Av
"Little Venice"
Harrow Road
Harrow Road
Western Avenue Extension
Royal Oak
Porchester Rd
Chepstow Rd
Bishop's Bridge Rd
Westbourne Grove

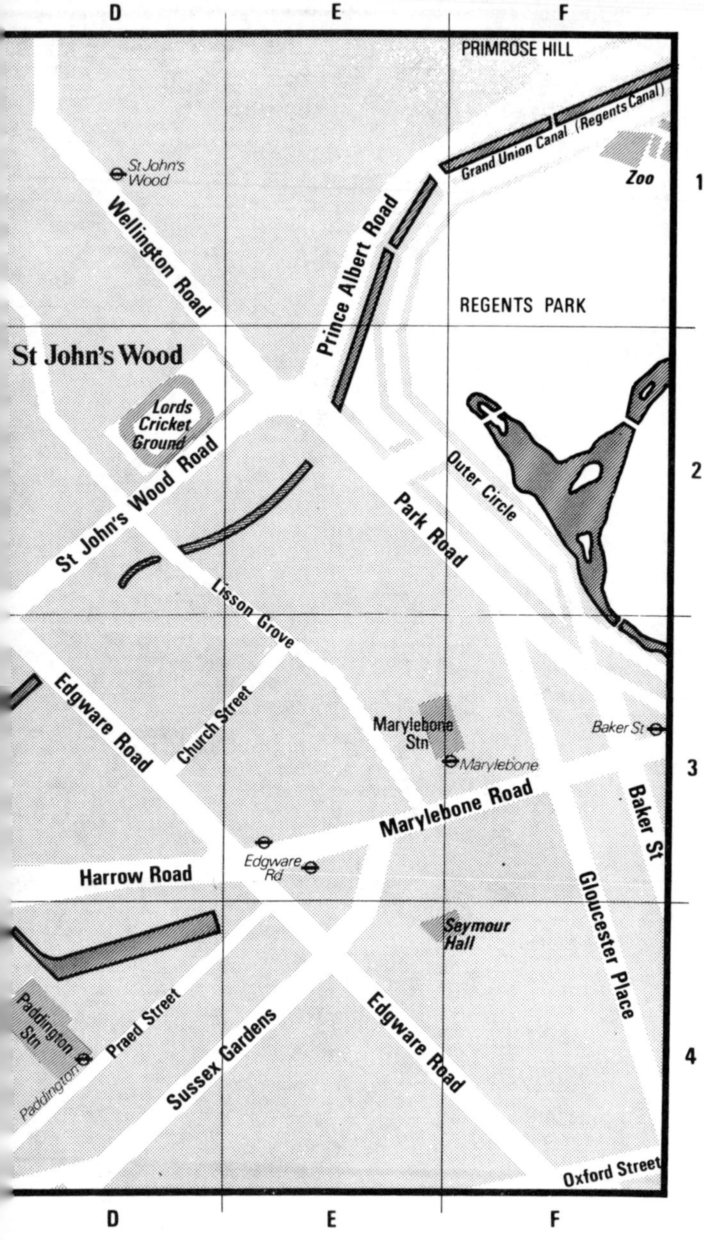
D
E
F
1
2
3
4
PRIMROSE HILL
Grand Union Canal (Regents Canal)
Zoo
St John's Wood
Wellington Road
Prince Albert Road
REGENTS PARK
St John's Wood
Lords Cricket Ground
St John's Wood Road
Outer Circle
Park Road
Lisson Grove
Edgware Road
Church Street
Marylebone Stn
Marylebone
Baker St
Baker St
Marylebone Road
Harrow Road
Edgware Rd
Gloucester Place
Seymour Hall
Paddington Stn
Paddington
Praed Street
Sussex Gardens
Edgware Road
Oxford Street

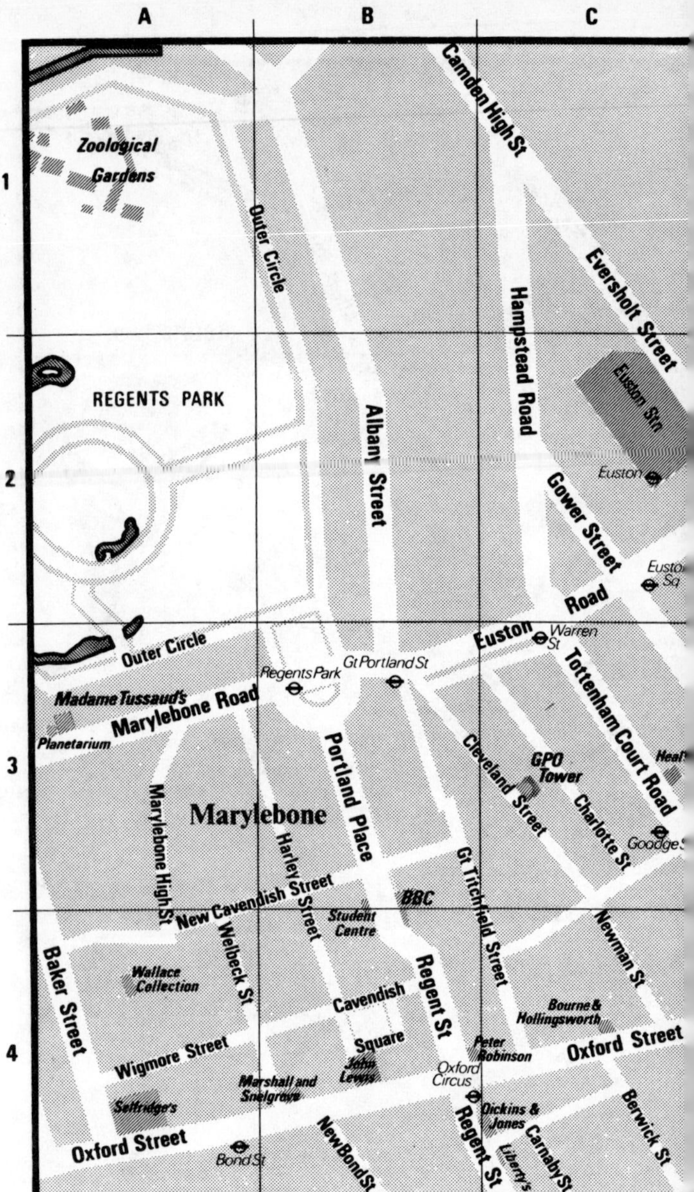
A
B
C
1
2
3
4
Zoological Gardens
Outer Circle
Camden High St
Eversholt Street
Hampstead Road
Euston Stn
Euston
REGENTS PARK
Albany Street
Gower Street
Euston Sq
Euston Road
Warren St
Outer Circle
Regents Park
Gt Portland St
Tottenham Court Road
Madame Tussaud's
Marylebone Road
Planetarium
Portland Place
Cleveland Street
GPO Tower
Charlotte St
Goodge St
Marylebone
Marylebone High St
Harley Street
Gt Titchfield Street
New Cavendish Street
BBC
Student Centre
Newman St
Baker Street
Wallace Collection
Welbeck St
Regent St
Cavendish Square
Bourne & Hollingsworth
Oxford Street
Wigmore Street
Peter Robinson
John Lewis
Oxford Circus
Marshall and Snelgrove
Selfridge's
Dickins & Jones
Berwick St
Oxford Street
Bond St
New Bond St
Regent St
Liberty's
Carnaby St

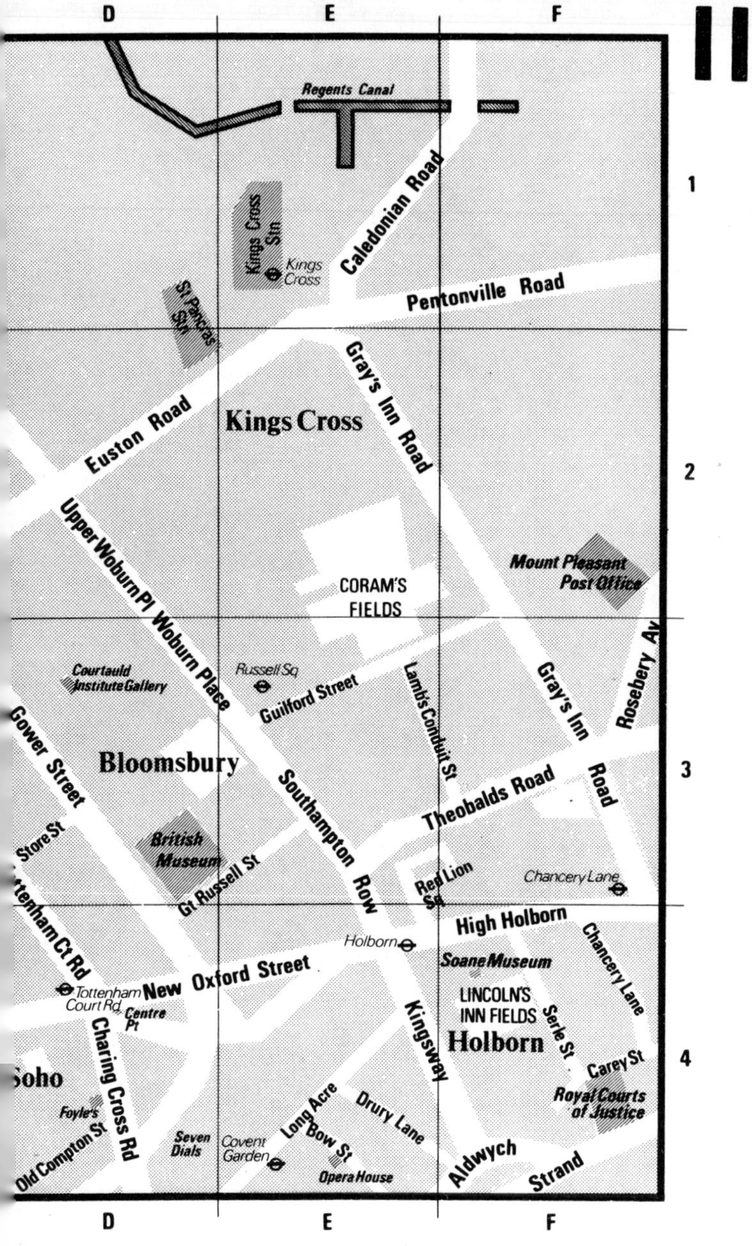
D
E
F
11
Regents Canal
Caledonian Road
Kings Cross Stn
Kings Cross
St Pancras Stn
Pentonville Road
Gray's Inn Road
Kings Cross
Euston Road
Upper Woburn Pl
Woburn Place
CORAM'S FIELDS
Mount Pleasant Post Office
Rosebery Av
Courtauld Institute Gallery
Russell Sq
Guilford Street
Lamb's Conduit St
Gray's Inn Road
Gower Street
Bloomsbury
Southampton Row
Theobalds Road
Store St
British Museum
Gt Russell St
Red Lion Sq
Chancery Lane
Tottenham Ct Rd
High Holborn
Holborn
Chancery Lane
Soane Museum
New Oxford Street
Tottenham Court Rd
Centre Pt
Kingsway
LINCOLN'S INN FIELDS
Serle St
Holborn
Charing Cross Rd
Soho
Carey St
Royal Courts of Justice
Foyle's
Long Acre
Drury Lane
Bow St
Old Compton St
Seven Dials
Covent Garden
Opera House
Aldwych
Strand
1
2
3
4

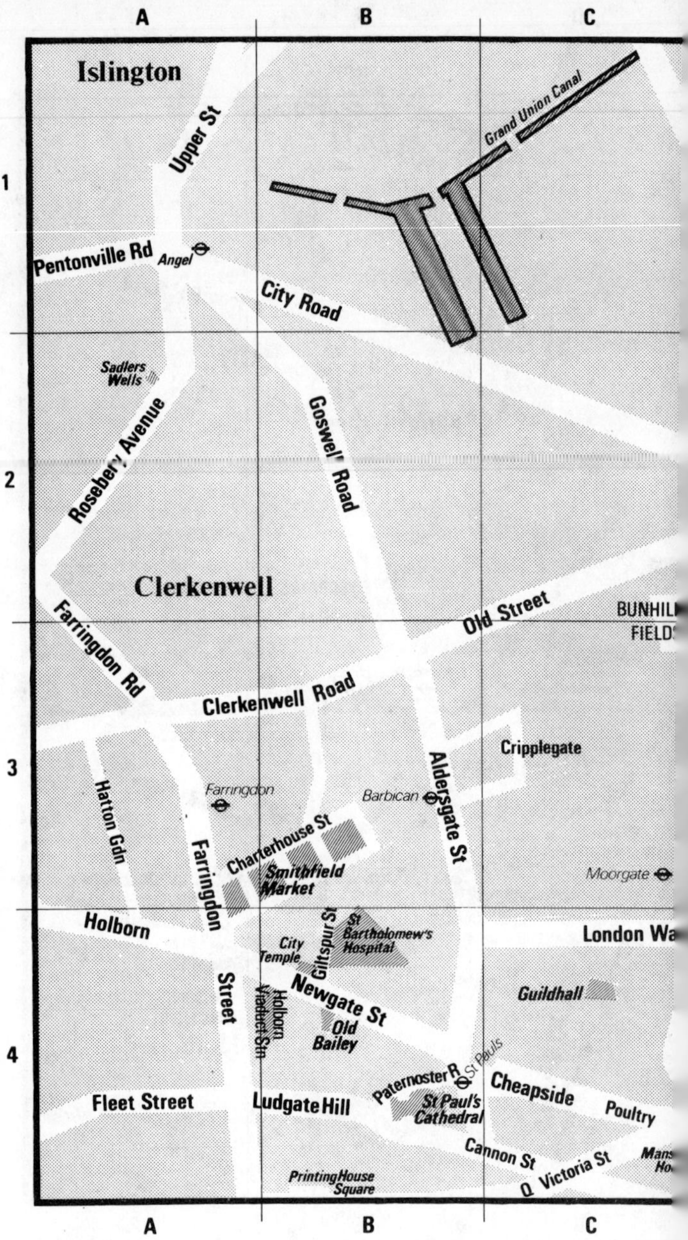

A
B
C
1
2
3
4
Islington
Upper St
Grand Union Canal
Pentonville Rd
Angel
City Road
Sadlers Wells
Rosebery Avenue
Goswell Road
Clerkenwell
Farringdon Rd
Old Street
BUNHILL FIELDS
Clerkenwell Road
Cripplegate
Hatton Gdn
Farringdon
Barbican
Aldersgate St
Charterhouse St
Smithfield Market
Farringdon
Moorgate
Holborn
Giltspur St
St Bartholomew's Hospital
City Temple
London Wa
Street
Holborn Viaduct Stn
Newgate St
Guildhall
Old Bailey
St Pauls
Paternoster R
Cheapside
Fleet Street
Ludgate Hill
St Paul's Cathedral
Poultry
Cannon St
Victoria St
PrintingHouse Square
A
B
C

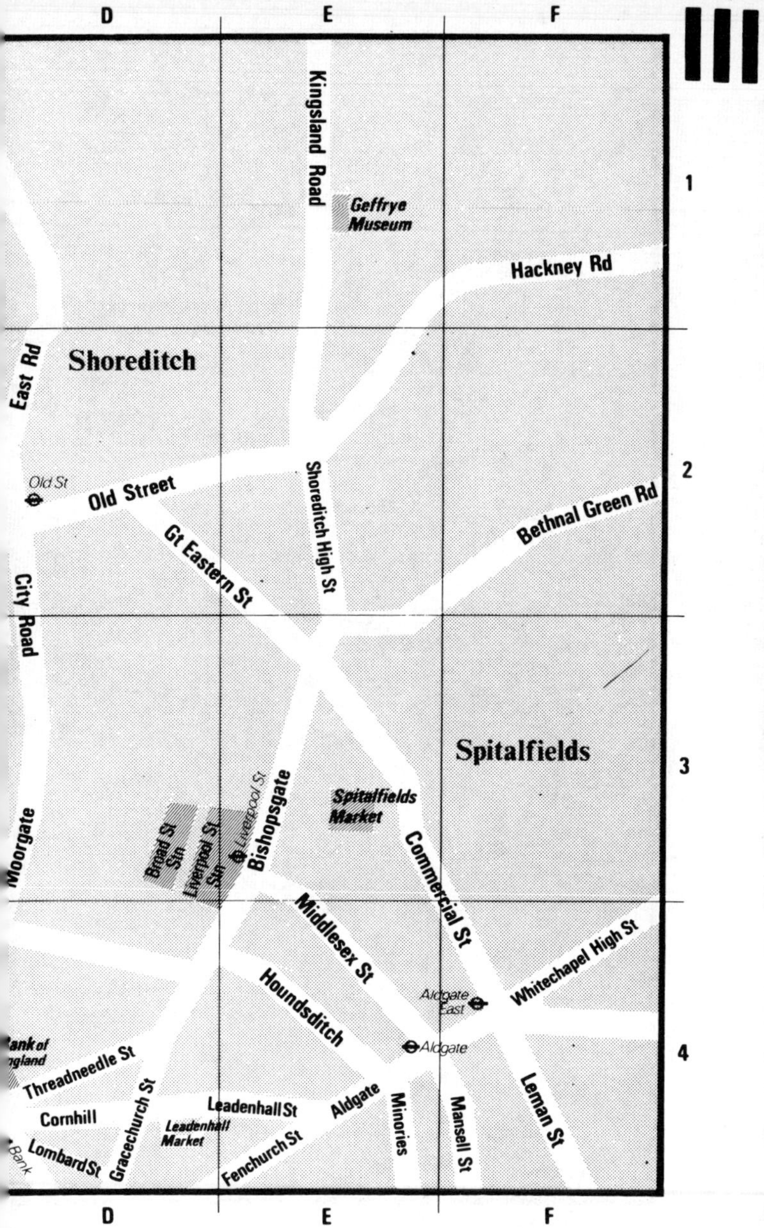
III
D
E
F
1
2
3
4
Kingsland Road
Geffrye Museum
Hackney Rd
Shoreditch
East Rd
Old St
Old Street
Shoreditch High St
Bethnal Green Rd
Gt Eastern St
City Road
Spitalfields
Spitalfields Market
Moorgate
Broad St Stn
Liverpool St Stn
Liverpool St
Bishopsgate
Commercial St
Middlesex St
Whitechapel High St
Houndsditch
Aldgate East
Aldgate
Threadneedle St
Cornhill
Lombard St
Bank
Gracechurch St
Leadenhall St
Leadenhall Market
Fenchurch St
Aldgate
Minories
Mansell St
Leman St
D
E
F

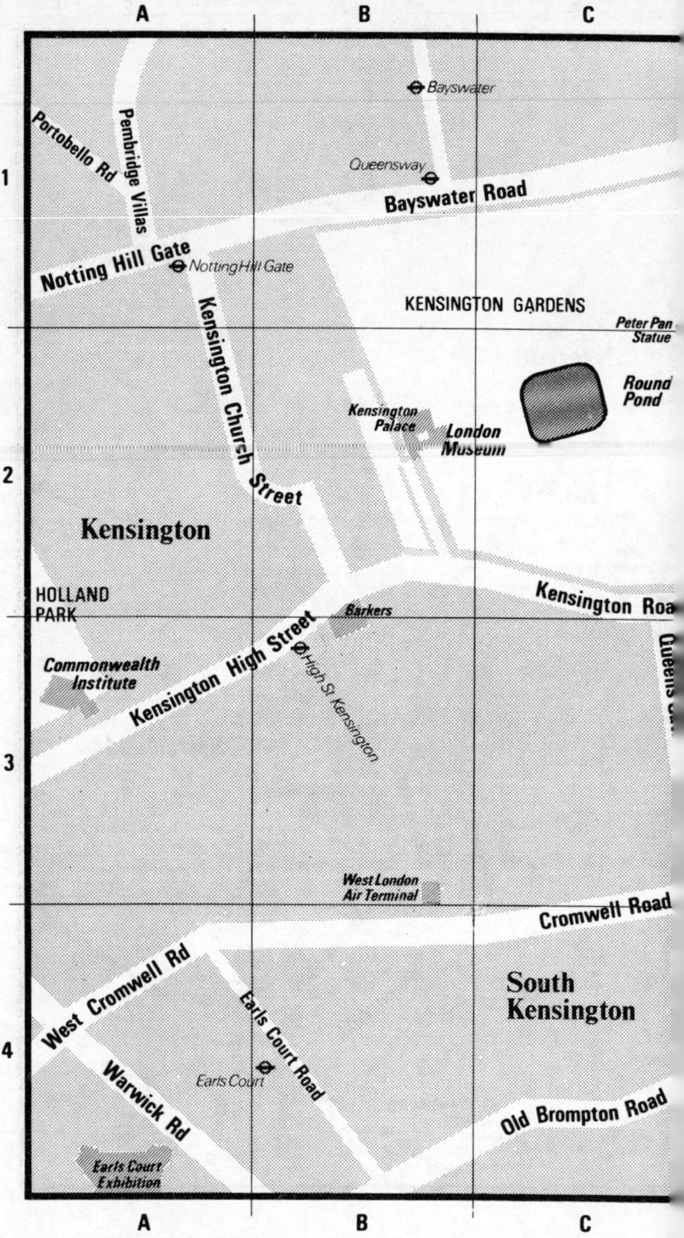

A
B
C
1
2
3
4
Bayswater
Queensway
Portobello Rd
Pembridge Villas
Bayswater Road
Notting Hill Gate
Notting Hill Gate
KENSINGTON GARDENS
Peter Pan Statue
Round Pond
Kensington Church Street
Kensington Palace
London Museum
Kensington
HOLLAND PARK
Kensington Road
Barkers
Commonwealth Institute
Kensington High Street
High St Kensington
West London Air Terminal
Cromwell Road
West Cromwell Rd
Earls Court Road
South Kensington
Warwick Rd
Earls Court
Old Brompton Road
Earls Court Exhibition

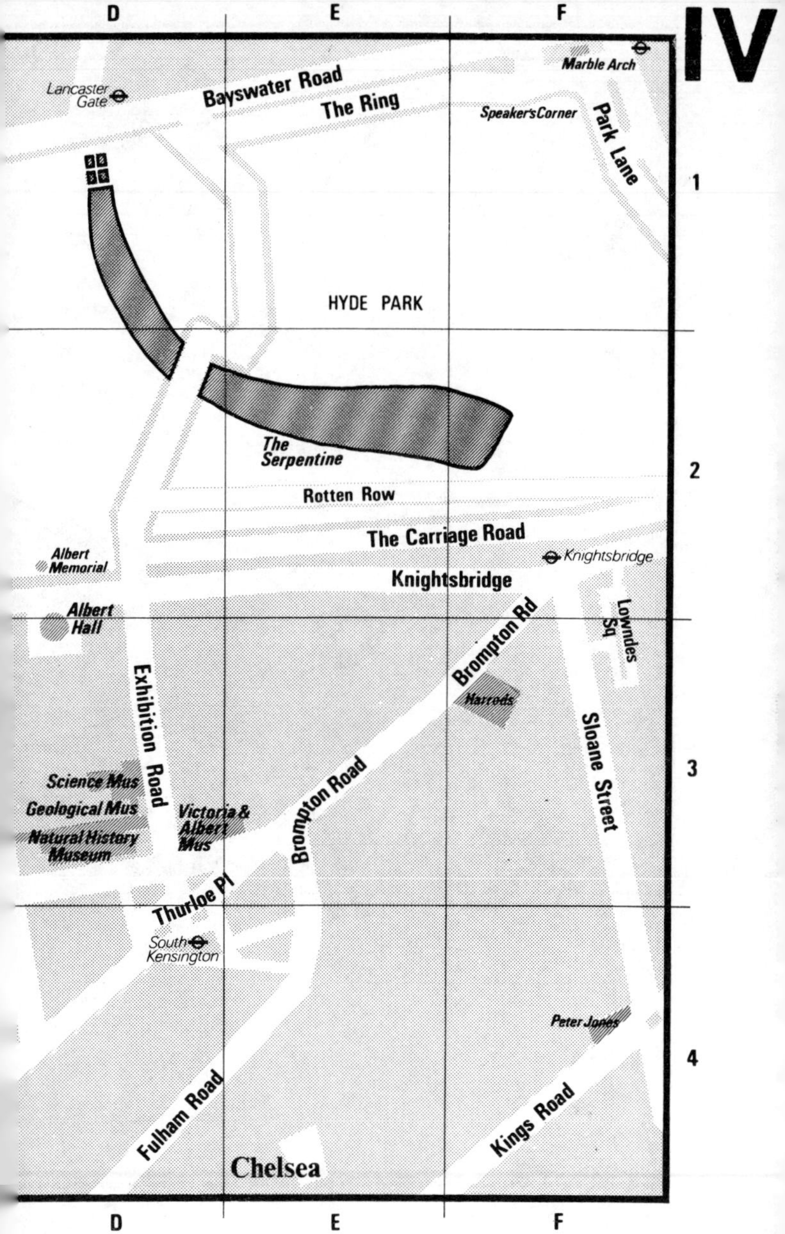

IV
D
E
F
1
2
3
4
Lancaster Gate
Bayswater Road
The Ring
Marble Arch
Speaker's Corner
Park Lane
HYDE PARK
The Serpentine
Rotten Row
The Carriage Road
Knightsbridge
Knightsbridge
Albert Memorial
Albert Hall
Lowndes Sq
Brompton Rd
Harrods
Exhibition Road
Sloane Street
Science Mus
Geological Mus
Natural History Museum
Victoria & Albert Mus
Brompton Road
Thurloe Pl
South Kensington
Peter Jones
Fulham Road
Kings Road
Chelsea

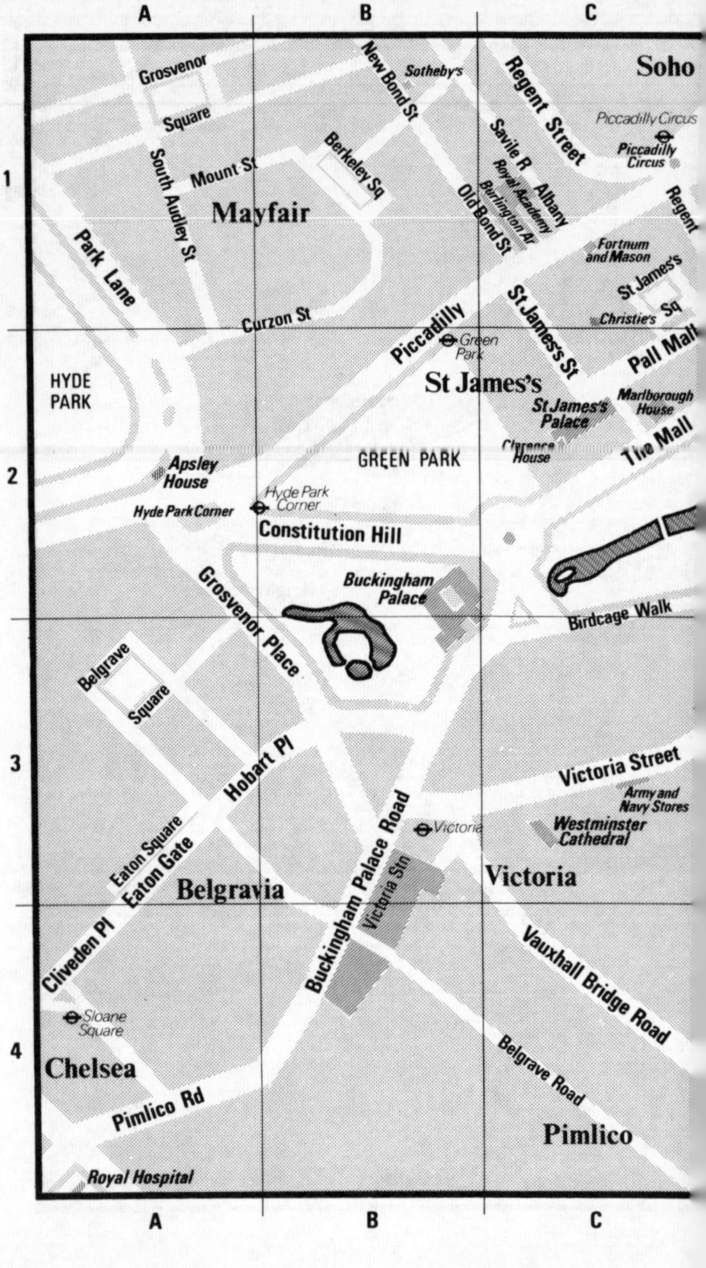

A
B
C
1
2
3
4
Soho
Grosvenor
Square
New Bond St
Sotheby's
Regent Street
Piccadilly Circus
Piccadilly Circus
Savile R
Royal Academy
Burlington Ar
Albany
Old Bond St
Regent
South Audley St
Mount St
Berkeley Sq
Mayfair
Park Lane
Fortnum and Mason
St James's Sq
Christie's
Curzon St
Piccadilly
Green Park
St James's St
Pall Mall
HYDE PARK
St James's
Marlborough House
St James's Palace
Clarence House
The Mall
GREEN PARK
Apsley House
Hyde Park Corner
Hyde Park Corner
Constitution Hill
Buckingham Palace
Grosvenor Place
Birdcage Walk
Belgrave Square
Hobart Pl
Victoria Street
Army and Navy Stores
Westminster Cathedral
Buckingham Palace Road
Victoria
Victoria Stn
Eaton Square
Eaton Gate
Belgravia
Victoria
Cliveden Pl
Vauxhall Bridge Road
Sloane Square
Chelsea
Belgrave Road
Pimlico Rd
Pimlico
Royal Hospital

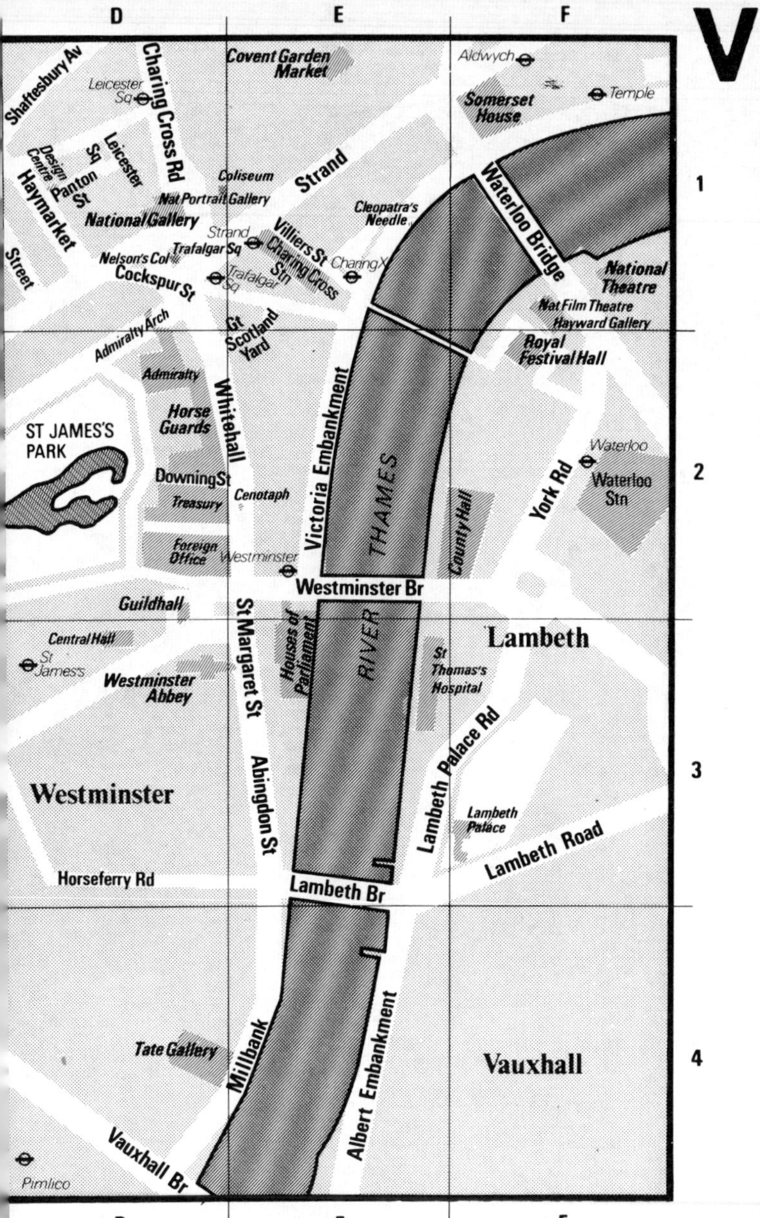

V
D
E
F
Covent Garden Market
Aldwych
Temple
Somerset House
Shaftesbury Av
Charing Cross Rd
Leicester Sq
Leicester Sq
Panton St
Design Centre
Haymarket
Coliseum
Strand
Nat Portrait Gallery
National Gallery
Cleopatra's Needle
Waterloo Bridge
Strand
Trafalgar Sq
Villiers St
Charing Cross Stn
Charing X
Nelson's Col
Cockspur St
Trafalgar Sq
Street
National Theatre
Nat Film Theatre
Hayward Gallery
Admiralty Arch
Gt Scotland Yard
Royal Festival Hall
Admiralty
Horse Guards
Whitehall
Victoria Embankment
ST JAMES'S PARK
Downing St
Treasury
Cenotaph
THAMES
County Hall
Waterloo
York Rd
Waterloo Stn
Foreign Office
Westminster
Westminster Br
Guildhall
St Margaret St
Houses of Parliament
RIVER
Lambeth
Central Hall
St James's
Westminster Abbey
St Thomas's Hospital
Lambeth Palace Rd
Abingdon St
Westminster
Lambeth Palace
Lambeth Road
Horseferry Rd
Lambeth Br
Millbank
Albert Embankment
Tate Gallery
Vauxhall
Vauxhall Br
Pimlico
1
2
3
4

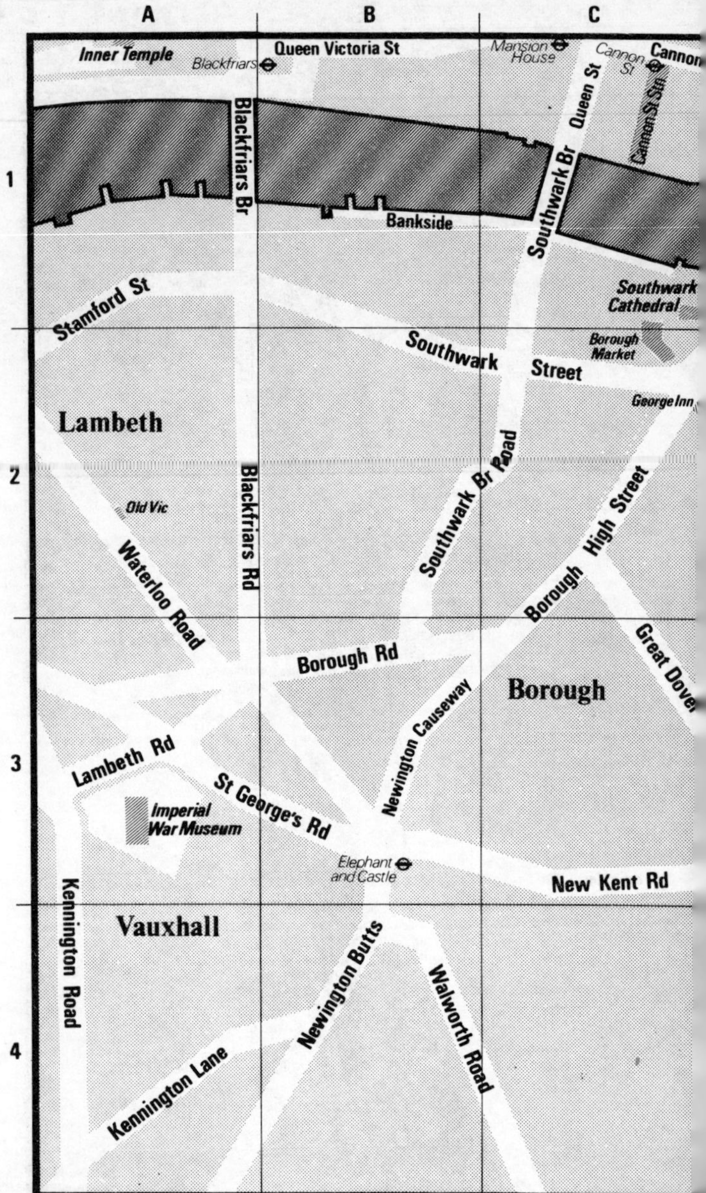
A
B
C
1
2
3
4
Inner Temple
Queen Victoria St
Blackfriars
Mansion House
Cannon St
Cannon
Queen St
Cannon St Stn
Blackfriars Br
Bankside
Southwark Br
Stamford St
Southwark Cathedral
Borough Market
Southwark Street
George Inn
Lambeth
Southwark Br Road
Borough High Street
Old Vic
Blackfriars Rd
Waterloo Road
Borough Rd
Great Dover
Borough
Newington Causeway
Lambeth Rd
St George's Rd
Imperial War Museum
Elephant and Castle
New Kent Rd
Kennington Road
Vauxhall
Newington Butts
Walworth Road
Kennington Lane

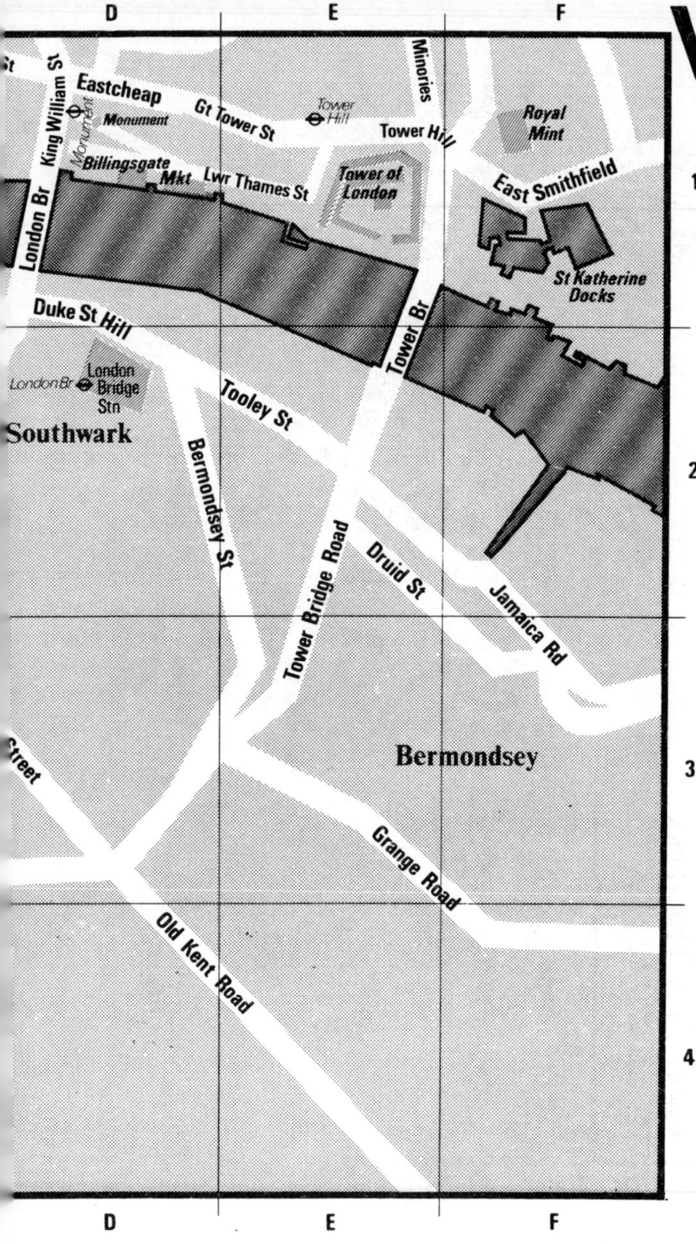
D
E
F
Eastcheap
King William St
Monument
Gt Tower St
Tower Hill
Minories
Tower Hill
Royal Mint
Billingsgate Mkt
Lwr Thames St
Tower of London
East Smithfield
London Br
St Katherine Docks
Duke St Hill
Tower Br
London Br
London Bridge Stn
Tooley St
Southwark
Bermondsey St
Tower Bridge Road
Druid St
Jamaica Rd
Street
Bermondsey
Grange Road
Old Kent Road
1
2
3
4
D
E
F

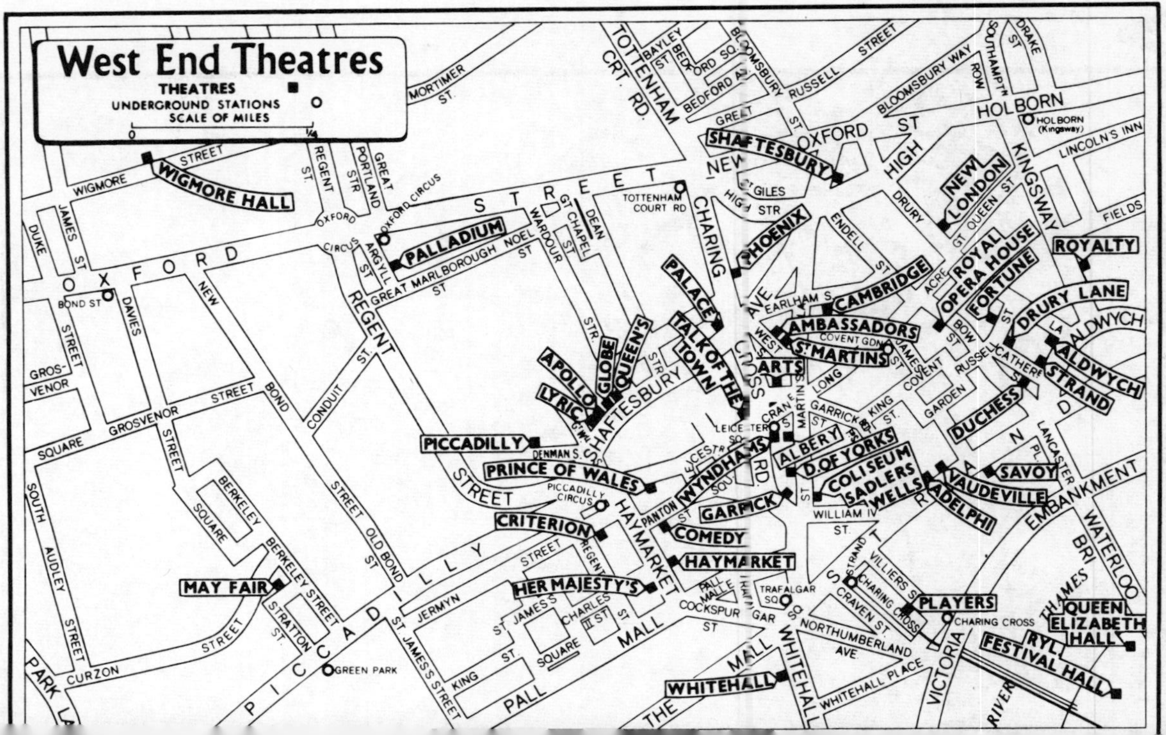
West End Theatres
THEATRES
UNDERGROUND STATIONS
SCALE OF MILES
0
1/4
WIGMORE HALL
PALLADIUM
PICCADILLY
PRINCE OF WALES
CRITERION
MAY FAIR
HER MAJESTY'S
APOLLO
LYRIC
GLOBE
QUEEN'S
PALACE
TALK OF THE TOWN
SHAFTESBURY
PHOENIX
CAMBRIDGE
AMBASSADORS
ST MARTINS
ARTS
WYNDHAMS
ALBERY
D. OF YORKS
COLISEUM
SADLERS WELLS
GARRICK
COMEDY
HAYMARKET
WHITEHALL
NEW LONDON
ROYAL OPERA HOUSE
FORTUNE
DRURY LANE
ROYALTY
ALDWYCH
STRAND
DUCHESS
SAVOY
VAUDEVILLE
ADELPHI
PLAYERS
QUEEN ELIZABETH HALL
RYL. FESTIVAL HALL
OXFORD CIRCUS
BOND ST
TOTTENHAM COURT RD
HOLBORN (Kingsway)
COVENT GDN
LEICESTER SQ
PICCADILLY CIRCUS
TRAFALGAR SQ
STRAND
CHARING CROSS
GREEN PARK

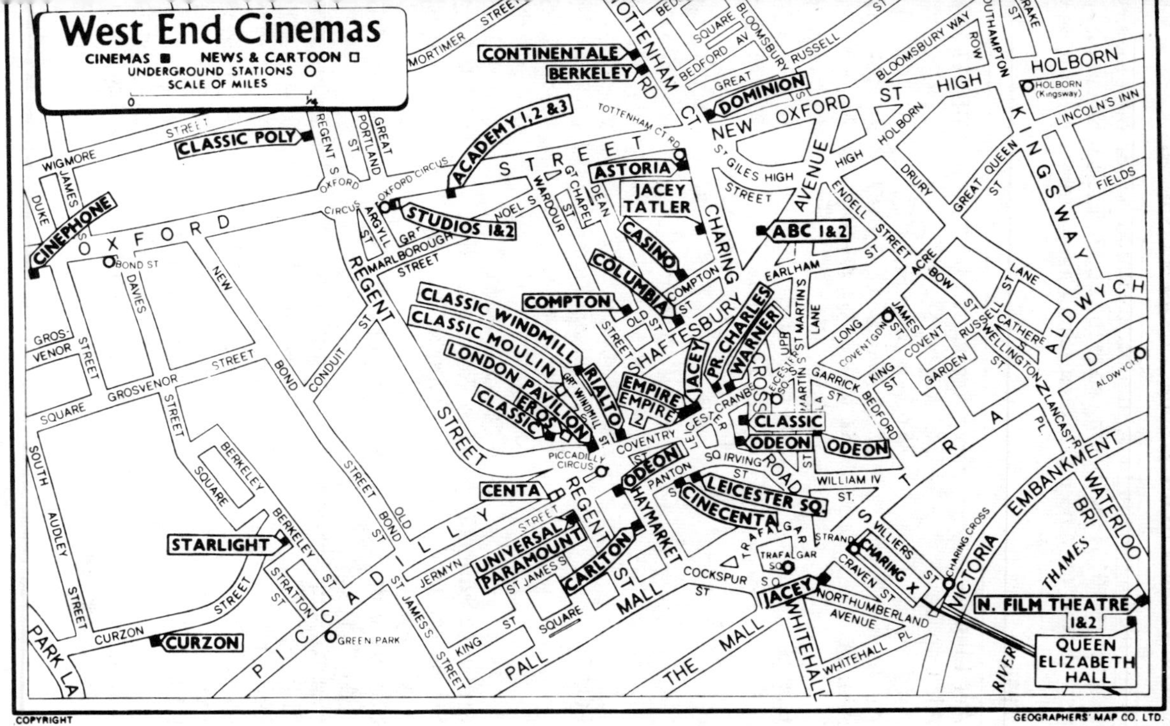
West End Cinemas
CINEMAS
NEWS & CARTOON
UNDERGROUND STATIONS
SCALE OF MILES
0
¼
CONTINENTALE
BERKELEY
DOMINION
CLASSIC POLY
ACADEMY 1,2 & 3
ASTORIA
JACEY TATLER
ABC 1&2
CINEPHONE
STUDIOS 1&2
CASINO
COLUMBIA
COMPTON
CLASSIC WINDMILL
CLASSIC MOULIN
LONDON PAVILION
EROS
CLASSIC
RIALTO
EMPIRE
EMPIRE 2
JACEY
PR. CHARLES
WARNER
CLASSIC
ODEON
ODEON
ODEON
CENTA
LEICESTER SQ.
CINECENTA
UNIVERSAL
PARAMOUNT
CARLTON
STARLIGHT
CURZON
JACEY
CHARING X
N. FILM THEATRE 1&2
QUEEN ELIZABETH HALL
OXFORD STREET
NEW OXFORD ST
HIGH HOLBORN
KINGSWAY
ALDWYCH
STRAND
CHARING CROSS ROAD
SHAFTESBURY AVENUE
REGENT STREET
PICCADILLY
HAYMARKET
PALL MALL
THE MALL
WHITEHALL
VICTORIA EMBANKMENT
RIVER THAMES
WATERLOO BRI
PICCADILLY CIRCUS
OXFORD CIRCUS
TRAFALGAR SQ
GREEN PARK
BOND ST
HOLBORN (Kingsway)
CHARING CROSS
ALDWYCH
COVENT GDN
TOTTENHAM CT RD
LEICESTER SQ
PARK LA
COPYRIGHT
GEOGRAPHERS' MAP CO. LTD.

Useful London Addresses and Telephone Numbers

When dialling any of these numbers, within London omit the firs two figures. 01 is the dialling code for London telephone number and should only be used when telephoning from country areas

Airlines

Aer Lingus	*223 Regent St., W1*	01-437 800
Air Canada	*142 Regent St., W1*	01-629 829
Air France	*158 New Bond St., W1*	01-499 951
Air India	*17/18 New Bond St., W1*	01-493 810
Alitalia	*251 Regent St., Oxford Circus, W1*	01-734 404
B.E.A.	*International*	01-370 541
	British Domestic	01-370 454
	Air Terminal, Cromwell Rd., SW3	01-370 425
	Lower Regent St., W1	01-370 541
	52 Grosvenor Gdns, SW1	01-370 541
	100 Cheapside, EC2	01-370 541
BOAC	*Air Terminal, Victoria, SW1*	01-834 446
	107 New Bond St., W1	01-834 232
	75 Regent St., W1	01-834 232
	62 Cheapside, EC2	01-834 232
British Caledonian	*65/67 Regent St., W1*	01-734 315
British Midland Airways	*33/39 Savile Row, W1*	01-734 010
Cambrian British Air Services	*457 The Strand, WC2*	01-839 676
East African Airways	*New Bond St., W1*	01-493 897
El Al	*185 Regent St., W1*	01-437 927
Finnair	*71 Regent St., W1*	01-734 527
Iberia	*169 Regent St., W1*	01-743 6351
JAL	*8 Hanover St., W1*	01-493 3271
KLM	*Time and Life Building, New Bond St., W1*	01-629 8803
Kuwait	*164 Piccadilly, W1*	01-499 7681
Lufthansa	*28 Piccadilly, W1*	01-437 9797

Luxair	*54 Regent St., W1*	01-734 0559
Middle East	*80 Piccadilly, W1*	01-493 5681
National	*81 Piccadilly, W1*	01-629 8272
Olympic	*141 New Bond St., W1*	01-493 7262
Pakistan International	*120 Regent St., W1*	01-734 5884
Pan Am	*193 Piccadilly, W1*	01-734 7292
Qantas	*Corner of Piccadilly and Old Bond St., W1*	01-629 9200
Sabena	*36 Piccadilly, W1*	01-437 6960
South African Airways	*251 Regent St., W1*	01-437 9621
SAS	*52 Conduit St., W1*	01-734 4020
Swissair	*Swiss Centre, 10 Wardour St., W1*	01-734 7931
TAP	*19 Regent St., W1*	01-734 4181
TWA	*200 Piccadilly, W1*	01-636 4090
UTA	*177 Piccadilly, W1*	01-493 4881
Varig	*235 Regent St., W1*	01-734 8981

Ballet

See "Opera and Ballet"

Car Hire

Avis Rent-A-Car	*35 Headfort Place, SW1*	01-245 9862
Hertz Rent-A-Car	*7 Herbrand St., WC1*	01-837 2898

Cinemas

ABC 1 & 2	*Shaftesbury Ave., W1*		01-836 8861
Academy One & Two	*165 Oxford St., W1*	One	01-437 2981
		Two	01-437 5129
Academy Three	*167 Oxford St., W1*		01-437 8819
Astoria	*157 Charing Cross Rd., WC2*		01-580 9562
Berkeley	*30a Tottenham Court Rd., W1*		01-636 8150
Bloomsbury	*Bernard St., WC1*		01-837 1177
Cameo Poly	*307 Regent St., W1*		01-580 1744

Cameo Royal	*32-35 Charing Cross Rd., WC2*	01-930 6915
Cameo Victoria	*152 Victoria St., SW1*	01-834 6588
Carlton	*Corner of Old Church St., King's Rd., SW3*	01-352 7488
Carlton	*Haymarket, SW1*	01-930 3711
Casino Cinerama	*Old Compton St., W1*	01-437 6877
Cinecenta	*Panton St., SW1*	01-930 0631
Cinephone	*429 Oxford St., W1*	01-629 4721
Classic	*98 Baker St., W1*	01-935 8836
Classic	*405 Kilburn High Rd., NW6*	01-624 6767
Classic	*Piccadilly Circus, W1*	01-437 2380
Classic	*Pond St., Hampstead, NW3*	01-794 4000
Classic Moulin	*43 Great Windmill St., Piccadilly Circus, W1*	01-437 1653
Columbia	*93 Shaftesbury Ave., W1*	01-734 5414
Continentale	*36 Tottenham Court Rd.,W1*	01-636 4193
Curzon	*Curzon St., W1*	01-499 3737
Dominion	*Tottenham Court Rd., W1*	01-580 9562
Empire	*Leicester Sq., WC2*	01-437 1234
Leicester Sq. Theatre	*Leicester Sq., WC2*	01-930 5252
London Pavilion	*3 Piccadilly Circus, W1*	01-437 2982
Metropole	*160 Victoria St., SW1*	01-834 0208
National Film Theatre	*South Bank, SE1*	01-928 3232
New Victoria	*17 Wilton Rd., SW1*	01-834 2544
Odeon	*Haymarket, SW1*	01-930 2738
Odeon	*Kensington High St., W8*	01-937 0131
Odeon	*Leicester Sq., WC2*	01-930 6111
Odeon	*Marble Arch, W1*	01-723 2011
Odeon	*St. Martin's Lane, WC2*	01-836 0691
Paramount	*Lower Regent St., Piccadilly, SW1*	01-839 6494
Paris Pullman	*65 Drayton Gdns., SW10*	01-373 5898
Prince Charles	*Leicester Sq., WC2*	01-437 8181
Rialto	*3 Coventry St., W1*	01-437 3488
Ritz	*Leicester Sq., WC2*	01-437 1234
Studio One	*225 Oxford St., W1*	01-437 3300
Studio Two	*225 Oxford St., W1*	01-437 3300

Universal	*Piccadilly Circus, SW1*	01-930 8944
Victoria	*Victoria Station, SW1*	01-834 7641
Warner	*Leicester Sq., WC2*	01-439 0791
Windmill	*17 Great Windmill St., W1*	01-437 7413

Credit Card Offices

American Express	*6 Haymarket, SW1*	01-930 4411
Diners Club	*214 Oxford St., W1*	01-499 4000

Concert Halls

Queen Elizabeth Hall	*South Bank, SE1*	01-928 3191
Royal Festival Hall	*South Bank, SE1*	01-928 3191
Wigmore Hall	*36 Wigmore St., W1*	01-935 2141

Opera and Ballet

Royal Opera House	*Covent Gdn., WC2*	01-240 1066
Sadler's Wells	*Roseberry Ave., EC1*	01-837 1672

Restaurants

A L'Ecu de France	*111 Jermyn St., SW1*	01-930 2837/8
Au Jardin des Gourmets	*5 Greek St., W1*	01-437 1816
Bentley's	*Swallow St., W1*	01-734 4756/6210
Berkeley Hotel	*Wilton Place, SW1*	01-235 6000
Boulestin	*25 Southampton St., WC2*	01-836 7061
Brompton Grill	*243 Brompton Rd., SW3 2EP*	01-589 8005
Cafe Royal	*68 Regent St., W1A 4TY*	01-930 2373
Caprice	*Arlington St., SW1*	01-493 5154
Carrier's	*2 Camden Passage, N1*	01-226 5353
Chez Ciccio	*38c Kensington Church St., W8*	01-937 2005
Chez Luba	*116 Draycott Ave., SW3*	01-584 0888
Chez Solange	*35 Cranbourn St., WC2*	01-836 5886/0542

Claridge's Hotel	*Brook St., W1*	01-629 8860
Connaught Hotel	*Carlos Place, W1*	01-499 7070
Coq d'Or	*Stratton St., W1*	01-629 7807
Dorchester Terrace	*Park Lane, W1*	01-629 8888
Etoile	*30 Charlotte St., W1*	01-636 7189
Grosvenor House	*Burghley Grill, Park Ln., W1*	01-499 6363
Hilton Roof	*Park Lane, W1*	01-493 8000
Hunting Lodge	*16 Lower Regent St., SW1*	01-930 4222/3
Hyde Park Hotel	*Knightsbridge, SW1*	01-235 2000
Isola Bella	*15 Frith St., W1*	01-437 3911/1656
Ivy	*1/5 West St., WC2*	01-836 4751
L'Aperitif	*Brown's Hotel, Dover St., W1*	01-493 6020
L'Escargot Bienvenu	*48 Greek St., W1*	01-437 4460
La Belle Meuniere	*5 Charlotte St., W1*	01-636 1134
Le Carrosse	*19/21 Elystan St., SW3*	01-584 5248
Le Chateaubriand	*May Fair Hotel, Berkeley St., W1*	01-629 7777
Martinez	*25 Swallow St., W1*	01-734 5066
Mirabelle	*56 Curzon St., W1*	01-499 4636
Overton's	*5 St. James's St., SW1*	01-839 3774
Prunier's	*72 St. James's St., SW1*	01-493 1373
Quaglino's	*16 Bury St., SW1*	01-930 6767
Ritz Hotel	*Piccadilly, W1*	01-493 8181
Rules	*35 Maiden Lane, WC2*	01-836 5314
Savoy Grill	*Strand, WC2*	01-836 4343
Scott's	*20 Mount St., W1*	01-629 5248
Simpson's in the Strand	*100 Strand, WC2*	01-836 9112
Stone's Chop House	*Panton St., SW1*	01-930 0037
The Empress	*15 Berkeley St., W1*	01-629 6126/7
Top of the Tower	*Maple St., W1*	01-636 3000
Trader Vic's	*22 Park Lane, W1*	01-493 7586
Vendome	*20 Dover St., W1*	01-629 5417
Westbury Hotel	*New Bond St., W1*	01-629 7755
Wheeler's	*Old Compton St., W1*	01-437 2706
White House	*Albany St., NW1*	01-387 1200
White Tower	*1 Percy St., W1*	01-636 8141

Theatres

Adelphi	*Strand, WC2*	01-836 7611
Aldwych	*Aldwych, WC2*	01-836 6404/5
Ambassadors	*West Street, WC2*	01-836 1171
Apollo	*Shaftesbury Ave., W1*	01-437 2663
Arts	*7 Great Newport St., WC2*	01-836 3334
Cambridge	*Earlham St., WC2H 9HU*	01-836 6056
Comedy	*Panton Street, SW1*	01-930 2578/9
Criterion	*Piccadilly Circus, W1*	01-930 3216
Duchess	*Catherine St., WC2*	01-836 8243
Duke of York's	*St. Martin's Lane, WC2N 4BG*	01-836 5122
Fortune	*Russell St., WC2*	01-836 2238
Garrick	*Charing Cross Rd., WC2H 0HH*	01-836 4601
Globe	*Shaftesbury Ave., W1*	01-437 1592/3
Haymarket	*Haymarket, SW1*	01-930 9832
Her Majesty's	*Haymarket, SW1*	01-930 6606
Lyric	*Shaftesbury Ave., W1*	01-437 3686/7
May Fair	*May Fair Hotel, W1*	01-629 3036
Mermaid	*Puddle Dock, EC4*	01-248 7656
National Theatre at Old Vic	*Waterloo Rd., SE1 8NB*	01-928 7616
New	*St. Martin's Lane, WC2*	01-836 3878
Palace	*Shaftesbury Ave., W1*	01-437 6834
Palladium	*Argyll St., W1*	01-437 7373
Phoenix	*Charing Cross Rd., WC2*	01-836 8611
Piccadilly	*Denman St., W1V 8DY*	01-437 4506
Prince of Wales	*Coventry St., W1*	01-930 8681
Queen's	*51 Shaftesbury Ave., W1*	01-734 1166
Royal Court	*Sloane Sq., SW1*	01-730 1745
Royal Opera House	*Covent Gdn., WC2E 7QA*	01-240 1066
Royal Festival Hall	*Belvedere Road, SE1*	01-928 3191
Sadler's Wells Opera	*The London Coliseum, St. Martin's Lane, WC2*	01-836 3161
St. Martin's	*West St., WC2*	01-836 1443
Savoy	*Strand, WC2*	01-836 8888

Shaftesbury	*Shaftesbury Ave., WC2*	01-836 6596
Strand	*Aldwych, WC2*	01-836 2660
Theatre Royal	*Drury Lane, WC2*	01-836 8108
Vaudeville	*Strand, WC2*	01-836 9988
Victoria Palace	*Victoria St., SW1*	01-834 1317
Westminster	*Palace St., SW1*	01-834 7882
Whitehall	*14 Whitehall, SW1*	01-930 6692
Wyndham's	*Charing Cross Rd., WC2H 0DA*	01-836 3028/9

Bookings

Keith Prowse	*155 Charing Cross Rd., WC2*	01-434 1171

Tourist Offices

British Tourist Auth.	*64 St. James St., SW1*	01-629 9191
London Tourist Infor.	*4 Grosvenor Gdns., SW1*	01-730 3400
American Express	See "Credit Cards"	
Thomas Cook & Son	*45 Berkeley St., W1*	01-499 4000

Index to People

Light number = Entry, Bold number = Page

Index to Places

Light number = Entry, Bold numbers = Pages and street number where applicable.